Christchurch Architecture

A Walking Guide

T0094684

John Walsh
Photography by Patrick Reynolds

MASSEY UNIVERSITY PRESS

To the architects and builders of Christchurch,
then and now.

CONTENTS

Introduction 5

A note about access and classifications 10

ROUTE 1: PARK SIDE 12

ROUTE 2: WEST BANK 60

ROUTE 3: EAST BANK 78

ROUTE 4: OLD CENTRE 102

ROUTE 5: NORTH SIDE 122

ROUTE 6: ILAM CAMPUS 142

A note about architectural styles 160

Glossary of architectural terms 164

Connections 166

Further reading 169

Acknowledgements 172

Index 173

INTRODUCTION

This book is a guide to a century and a half of Christchurch architecture, presenting outstanding examples of the various styles that have been in vogue, and introducing the significant architects who have practised in the city. It focuses on the centre of the city — the area bounded by the 'Four Avenues': Bealey, Fitzgerald, Moorhouse and Deans — and the important architectural site that is the Ilam campus of the University of Canterbury. This is where the city's most significant buildings can be seen and, in many cases, visited.

Of New Zealand's four main cities, Christchurch is the most conscious of its architectural history. Such civic awareness made the loss of much — but by no means all — of Christchurch's architectural legacy in and after the earthquakes of 2010–2011 even more poignant, and the debates about reconstruction even more pointed. This is a city that cares about its buildings.

The history of Christchurch architecture is a coherent and legible narrative, or at least it was, before the earthquakes. It dovetails with the wider story of the city's gestation and development; from the start, Christchurch's architecture has been a key component of the city's Anglocentric brand. Christchurch began as an intentional city: it was founded in the 1850s by people with a vision for an ideal settlement and a plan for its realisation. That plan really was a plan — a grid imposed on a stretch of flat land (and on other people who had long used that land, of which more later). Christchurch was conceived as an Anglican colony, a transplanted cross-section of English society, and the settlers wasted no time in replicating the institutions of established Victorian order and in constructing the buildings to house them.

The regnant architectural style of the settlement moment was Gothic Revival, which was closely associated with

Anglicanism in mid-nineteenth-century England. Gothic Revival was the original style of the Christchurch settlement and dominated the religious, governmental and institutional architecture of the city until the end of the nineteenth century. The style's leading local exponent was Benjamin Mountfort, a figure who towers over the first 40 years of Christchurch architecture. (Ten of the buildings in this guide were totally or partially designed by Mountfort.) Christchurch architecture has had two outstanding eras, periods in which the city's two greatest architects were producing their best work and, at the time, the best buildings in the country. Mountfort's Gothic Revival heyday, from the mid-1860s to the mid-1880s, was the first period of Christchurch architectural pre-eminence; the second was the years from the mid-1950s to the early 1970s, when Miles — later Sir Miles — Warren was engaged in his Brutalist phase.

Mountfort had able contemporaries, if not peers, architects such as ecclesiastical specialist Robert Speechly, a short-term migrant, and William Barnett Armson, Christchurch's prototypical successful architect-businessman. Warren, too, had talented contemporaries, none more important than his long-time practice partner, Maurice Mahoney. From the 1950s through the 1970s, Christchurch had a strong Modernist architectural scene, populated by architects such as — to cite just those whose work features in this book — Paul Pascoe, Humphrey Hall, Keith Mackenzie, Holger Henning-Hansen, and the architects who worked in anonymity for the Ministry of Works. ('Full many a gem of purest ray serene / The dark unfathom'd caves of ocean bear' — Thomas Gray might have been thinking of Ministry architects when he wrote his 'Elegy'.) And then there was Peter Beaven. Like planets in a small solar system, Beaven and Warren spun around on orbits that sometimes came into volatile proximity. Perhaps a chivalric analogy is more appropriate: especially in the twilight of their careers, Warren and Beaven often jousted over Christchurch heritage and urban issues, one entering the lists as a knight of the realm, the other as an indomitable Don Quixote.

A ribbon of design talent runs through the history of Christchurch architecture, connecting the eras of Mountfort and Warren. In the 80 years from late-career Mountfort to early-career Warren the city's most notable architects were Samuel Hurst Seager and Cecil Wood, although John Collins and Richard Harman had long careers in the decades before the Second World War, and the England and Luttrell brothers were also prominent in the early twentieth century. Between High Gothic Revivalism and Brutalist Modernism, Christchurch architects sampled the regularly replenished smorgasbord of styles on offer in the Anglophone world. The city was treated to buildings in the Italianate, Collegiate Gothic, 'Tudorbethan', Queen Anne Revival and neo-Georgian styles, before Art Deco and Spanish Mission made their appearance. Continuity amidst this change was provided by a tradition of masonry construction and a genealogical design consciousness. Even as central Christchurch became a city of Modernist concrete, its architects alluded to its days of neo-Gothic stone, adding pointy bits to Brutalist buildings.

Some of the most important buildings from the 1860s to the 1970s have been carefully restored after the 2010–2011 earthquakes — the Great Hall at the Christchurch Arts Centre, for example, and the Memorial Dining Room at Christ's College and Christchurch Town Hall. Other historic buildings have gone forever, most notably the Italian Renaissance-style Cathedral of the Blessed Sacrament (Francis William Petre, 1905), with its dome that evoked the Duomo (in Florence, that is). Peter Beaven liked to cite George Bernard Shaw's praise of Christchurch's cathedral, taking mischievous delight in mimicking the locals' penny-dropping awareness that their distinguished visitor was referring not to the Anglican cathedral in the centre of the city but to the Catholic one down by the gasworks.

History, even aside from seismic events, has not been kind to Christchurch buildings designed between the end of Modernism and the eve of the earthquakes. Post-modern architecture was always a bit of a freak show, everywhere, but Christchurch got off relatively lightly. Instead, the city's architectural problem, in the late twentieth and early twenty-first centuries, was the increasingly moribund condition of the inner city. With a few exceptions, if you wanted to see good new architecture in Christchurch, in the millennium-ending decades, you headed to the suburbs to look at houses.

Things have improved in central Christchurch since the difficult years immediately following the earthquakes. There are still many gaps in city streetscapes and a profusion of empty lots, and a rash of ubiquitous tilt-slab concrete and glass buildings has provided critics with an itch to scratch, but the government investment in 'anchor' projects and the local determination to save significant heritage buildings are reviving the central city. The quality of many of these buildings, both new and conserved, not just in a design sense but also in terms of environmental and social performance, is a cause for civic optimism.

It is not a coincidence that the raising of architectural consciousness in Christchurch is contemporaneous with the increasing prominence in the city's economic life of the local iwi, Ngāi Tahu. The city of Christchurch was established in a place that already was a place — Ōtautahi was its name — and the wealth of Canterbury Province stemmed from the 1848 alienation, via a payment of £2000, of 20 million acres of Ngāi Tahu land. No Māori iwi has been more successful than Ngāi Tahu in using the Waitangi Treaty settlement process to develop the economic resources necessary to influence not just the politics but also the shaping of a city. As some of the projects in this guide indicate, Ngāi Tahu are regaining their naming rights to Ōtautahi-Christchurch, and design influence is starting to follow.

On the subject of inclusivity, there is another point to make. Readers of this guide will not fail to notice that it is a chronicle of the works of white males, not all of them dead.

Architecture in Christchurch, as in most places, has been, until very recently, a gendered profession. Without being glib, it is to be hoped that the events that have shaken up Christchurch might have the positive effect of sufficiently disturbing the structures of the architectural profession to make room for women in the architectural story of the city.

A NOTE ABOUT ACCESS AND CLASSIFICATIONS

This book is a footpath guide to the architecture of central Christchurch, but many of the buildings and sites are open to closer inspection, and more may become accessible when post-earthquake repairs are completed.

Route 1: Like the surrounding Hagley Park, the Christchurch Botanic Gardens Visitor Centre is open to the public every day (and has a café), and Christ's College offers tours of its campus which can be booked on the school's website. Much of the campus of the Christchurch Arts Centre can be explored, and there are several cafés in and around the site.

Route 2: Oi Manawa Canterbury Earthquake National Memorial is designed as a site to be walked through and the Bridge of Remembrance is a functioning pedestrian thoroughfare. Te Hononga Christchurch Civic Building is open to the public on weekdays, while Toi Moroki Centre of Contemporary Art (CoCA) Gallery and Christchurch Art Gallery Te Puna o Waiwhetū are open every day.

Route 3: The Post and Telegraph Office has been converted into commercial premises and includes a café, and the public are encouraged to use the laneways that run through the Stranges and Glendenning Hill Building and service several hospitality venues. Hine-Pāka Christchurch Bus Interchange is a public waiting, if not loitering, space, and Oxford Terrace is a destination for drinkers and diners.

Route 4: It will be years before ChristChurch Cathedral will be open to visitors, but the 'Cardboard' Cathedral is open to the public during the week, and to Anglican worshippers on Sundays. (Check the website for opening and service times.)

Tākaro ā Poi Margaret Mahy Family Playground is designed for children but welcomes visitors of all ages. Oxford Terrace Baptist Church welcomes members of that confessional group to its services. New Regent Street is a public street with many cafés and restaurants. Isaac Theatre Royal stages performances which may be booked on the venue's website. Tūranga Christchurch Central Library is open to the public every day, keeping longer hours on weekdays.

Route 5: Knox Church is open to Presbyterian worshippers and, no doubt, sympathetic believers on Sundays. (Details on the church's website.) Victoria Clock Tower is on a traffic island but can be reached on foot. Christchurch Town Hall is a performance venue. (Tickets may be booked on the Town Hall website.) St Mary's Convent (Rose) Chapel is now run as an events venue.

Route 6: The University of Canterbury's Ilam campus is publicly accessible, although not all buildings are open to visitors. There are cafés at various sites around the campus, including the Ernest Rutherford Building.

Many of the buildings in this guide are listed as Historic Places (Category 1 or 2). These appellations are applied by Heritage New Zealand, the government agency that identifies New Zealand's important historical and cultural heritage sites. Category 1 Historic Places are those of special or outstanding historical or cultural significance; Category 2 Historic Places have historical or cultural significance (but are not so special). It should be noted that heritage listing does not guarantee heritage protection.

ROUTE 1:
PARK SIDE

The planned foundation of Christchurch bequeathed two great legacies to the city: in the natural environment, Hagley Park and the Botanic Gardens; in the built environment, Gothic Revival architecture. This route along the west side of the CBD, and into the eastern edge of Hagley Park, includes two of the strongest architectural compositions in the city: the buildings around the Christ's College quadrangle, and the former Canterbury University buildings that now constitute The Arts Centre. The route ends near one of the four squares incorporated in the original city plan, this one named for the sixteenth-century English Protestant martyr Thomas Cranmer.

Hagley Community College Main Building

510 Hagley Avenue

George Penlington, 1924
Historic Place Category 2

The main building at Hagley Community College (formerly West Christchurch School) suggests the architecture of English private schools. Its style is neo-Georgian, with a Queen Anne inflection: sedate and symmetrical, built of brick with masonry quoins at the edges, a pediment and flagpole in the middle, and Ionic columns framing the main entrance. So far, so traditional, but looks can deceive. Despite the appearance of its main building, Hagley Community College sits at the progressive end of the New Zealand state education system — 'no one wears a uniform and everyone's on a first name basis,' the school's website declares. And, when you look more closely, the building itself is, modestly, heterodox. The proportions are disciplined but also a little out of order — the main façade is really one big framed window. When new, West Christchurch School was a breath of fresh air, a modern learning environment of its time. George Penlington (1865–1932), chief architect of the Canterbury Education Board — for most of the twentieth century public education was run by regional boards — designed the building to meet New Zealand's first school building code, which addressed post-First World War concerns about national health and hygiene by mandating standards for natural light and ventilation.

Hagley Oval Pavilion

South Hagley Park, 57 Riccarton Avenue

Athfield Architects, 2014

For a century, from the bewhiskered decades of the late 1800s to the more socially heterogeneous late twentieth century, (men's) cricket dominated the summer half of New Zealand's sporting calendar. Rugby, of course, got winter pretty much all to itself. This season-based sporting duopoly allowed for ground-sharing arrangements in the country's cities and towns. In Christchurch, where cricket has always been particularly strong — the first club was formed just six months after the arrival of the 'First Four Ships' in December 1850 — the sport, at its inter-provincial and international levels, co-existed with rugby at Lancaster Park, until rugby pushed its season into late summer in the 1990s. In response to rugby's manspreading, and the decline in cricket crowds, cricket administrators decided to shift to a new 'boutique' venue in Hagley Park. The proposal was controversial because Hagley Park, according to its 1855 foundation ordinance, was 'to be reserved forever as a public park'. Establishment cricket got its way, via the Environment Court, and the result is a very pleasant venue that can accommodate 12,000 spectators on the oval's grassy raised banks and in the pavilion designed by Trevor Watt of Athfield Architects. The signature gesture is the pavilion's tensioned fabric roof, a series of tent forms with a familial relationship to the Mound Stand (Michael Hopkins & Partners, 1987) at Lord's Cricket Ground in London.

Christchurch Botanic Gardens Visitor Centre

Rolleston Avenue

Patterson Associates, 2014

The most fortunate legacy of Christchurch's gestation as a planned settlement is the extensive reserve on the west side of the central city. Most of this greenbelt — 185 hectares — is given over to the woodland and playing fields of Hagley Park, but since 1863 another 21 hectares, circumscribed by a loop of the Avon River, have been occupied by the Christchurch Botanic Gardens. Half a dozen conservatories were built in the Gardens in the twentieth century; in 2014, they were joined by the Visitor Centre designed by Patterson Associates. The granting of such a notable Christchurch civic commission to an Auckland-based architecture practice was perhaps surprising — in architecture, as with other pursuits, Canterbury has a tradition, often justified, of provincial preference — but the outcome justified the adventure. The Visitor Centre, which includes a café, shop, library, exhibition space and plant propagation areas, was one of the city's first earthquake recovery projects. In designing the building, Patterson Associates celebrated the traditional form of its function — the Visitor Centre is adapted from a Dutch commercial greenhouse construction system — in a rhythmic march of modular units and saw-tooth roofs. Inside, it's also white but not quite as bright as natural light filtered through fritted glass plays on patterned concrete walls and ceilings.

Canterbury Museum

Rolleston Avenue at Worcester Boulevard

Benjamin Mountfort, 1870–1882
Historic Place Category 1

Canterbury Museum is a monument to two of New Zealand's eminent Victorians, and to the collecting and taxonomic mania of their age. Institutionally, the museum owes a significant foundational debt to its inaugural director, Julius von Haast (1822–1987); architecturally, the credit belongs to Benjamin Mountfort (1825–1898). Haast, a boundlessly energetic and ambitious scion of the Prussian bourgeoisie with a geology degree from the Rhenish Friedrich Wilhelm University Bonn, was commissioned in 1858 by an English shipping company to go to New Zealand and report on the prospects for German emigration. His arrival at the end of the year was coincident with that of the Austrian geologist Ferdinand von Hochstetter (1829–1884) and Haast helped Hochstetter undertake the first geological survey of New Zealand. Haast then pursued a career as a mapper, prospecting geologist and all-round scientific explorer. He was an inveterate collector of geological and zoological specimens; in the mid-1860s, he alighted eagerly on some spectacular discoveries — moa bones, which he trafficked to European museums, and a skeleton of the extinct Hieraaetus moorei, or Haast's eagle. (Possessed of a sizeable ego, Haast would have been gratified that his name was attached to the world's largest raptor.) In 1861 Haast started his own small museum in Christchurch and then advocated successfully for a public museum. A design competition yielded two winning entries, those of Robert Speechly (1840–1884) and Benjamin Mountfort, before the Provincial Government awarded the project to the Provincial Engineer, Edward Dobson (1816/17–1908), who was Haast's father-in-law. After some now-obscure political manoeuvring, Mountfort re-captured the commission, designing a stone building (1870) and, over the next dozen years, three extensions, all generally cleaving to the architect's signature Gothic Revival style. The museum was further extended in 1958 and 1977 and seismically strengthened. In the early 2000s, a renovation design by Athfield Architects, defended by Sir Miles Warren, was stymied by heritage resisters, led by Peter Beaven. The building survived the 2010–2011 earthquakes in good shape.

Canterbury Museum, Rolleston Avenue.

The Arts Centre
Te Matatiki Toi Ora

The Arts Centre Te Matatiki Toi Ora is a complex of 23 buildings, 21 of which are listed as Historic Place Category 1. Constructed between the 1870s and the 1920s, the buildings were all designed to serve an educational purpose. Most housed the various departments and facilities of Canterbury College, the precursor of the University of Canterbury, which was founded in 1873, although two of the buildings were originally a girls' and a boys' public high school. Over the half century of construction on the College's central city site, the institution and its architects stayed loyal to the foundational Gothic Revival style initiated by Benjamin Mountfort (1825–1898). The result is a remarkably coherent collection of buildings which expresses the Oxbridge educational aspirations of the Anglican Canterbury settlement. The roll-call of architects who worked at Canterbury College is a who's who of late nineteenth- and early twentieth-century Christchurch architecture: Mountfort; William Barnett Armson (1832/33–1883); Thomas Cane (1830–1905); Samuel Hurst Seager (1855–1933); John James Collins (1855–1933); Richard Dacre Harman (1859–1927). Only Cecil Wood didn't get a look in. Heritage campaigners helped save the College buildings after the university decamped to suburban Ilam in the 1960s and '70s, and the campus has been converted into an arts and cultural venue. The buildings were damaged significantly in the 2010–2011 earthquakes; restoration has been extensive and expensive. The regret that the university, and the city, lost something through the Ilam diaspora has never gone away; lately, in a reverse migration, the university's music school and classics department have returned to the original campus.

A Christchurch Boys' High School

B Clock Tower Block

C Great Hall

D Chemistry Laboratory

E Library

Great Hall (left) and West Lecture Building (Collins and Harman, 1917). The Arts Centre Te Matatiki Toi Ora, Rolleston Avenue side

Christchurch Boys' High School

William Barnett Armson, 1881
Historic Place Category 1

Christchurch Boys' High School, interestingly, was founded a few years after the adjacent Christchurch Girls' High School (Thomas Cane, 1878) and, like its neighbour, served as a feeder school to parent institution Canterbury College. The basalt and limestone Boys' High included teachers' rooms, a swimming pool, a fives court and the 'Big Room' used for assemblies and teaching. This room, it seems, quickly gained a reputation for disorderly behaviour. In 1883, a government inspector opined that 'perhaps there was a little too much anxiety to produce an elegant building and too little care taken to make it thoroughly suitable for school pupils'. This verdict would not have amused the building's architect, William Barnett Armson (1832/33–1883), if indeed he was still alive to read it. According to historian Jonathan Mane-Wheoki, Armson was a meticulous draughtsman who 'operated at a level of professionalism rare in New Zealand at that time', but the 'short, tubby and slightly bald' architect could be brusque with officials, clients and builders. Armson was raised in Melbourne, came to Dunedin in 1862, and spent five years on the West Coast designing banks, churches and hotels before settling in Christchurch in 1870. Armson was prolific and stylistically fluent: many of his buildings were Italianate, but he had no trouble conforming to Canterbury College's Gothic Revival norm. Boys' High School received several additions before outgrowing its site and moving from the Canterbury College campus in the mid-1920s.

Clock Tower Block

Benjamin Mountfort, 1877
Historic Place Category 1

In the generation following the arrival of the Canterbury
Association settlers in Christchurch in 1850, the colonists
set about developing the institutions necessary to produce a
facsimile of English society, minus an hereditary aristocracy at
the top and a lumpenproletariat at the bottom. In quick order,
the settlers built an Anglican church, founded a boys' school
(Christ's College) and a hospital, laid the foundations for a
cathedral (although, as in many places, cathedral completion
has been something of a Sisyphean task), and established
provincial government. They also started newspapers,
gentlemen's and cricket clubs, a horticulture society, and a
museum. All this busyness, the colony's planners recognised,
required some adjunct intellectual capacity. From the start,
the Canterbury Association intended that education in the
settlement would culminate in a tertiary level. In 1873,
therefore, the Canterbury College Board of Governors
announced a competition to design the College's buildings.
The competition was won by Benjamin Mountfort, and the
first College building to be constructed was the Clock Tower
block. This building debuted the College's architectural
genre — Gothic Revivalism, the house style of nineteenth-
century Anglicanism, and Mountfort's forte. If you wanted
an emblematic Victorian building type, apart from the
church, it would be hard to ignore the clock tower. The
Canterbury College clock tower served the practical purpose
of hastening students to their classes. It also sent a moral
message: for the purposeful Victorians, time was a resource
that was not to be wasted.

Great Hall

Benjamin Mountfort, 1882
Historic Place Category 1

The Great Hall was part of Benjamin Mountfort's competition-winning design for Canterbury College and it shows an architect at the height of his powers. By the time he designed the Great Hall, Mountfort had been in Christchurch for 30 years, having arrived as one of the original Canterbury Association settlers in 1850. He had received his architectural training, and ideological shaping, in London from Richard Cromwell Carpenter (1812–1855), a member of High Church Anglicanism's de facto architectural wing, the Ecclesiological Society. (The Society promoted the revival of both the religious ritual and Gothic architecture of the medieval church.) In Christchurch, Mountfort overcame an early setback — he made the rookie mistake of using unseasoned timber in a church in Lyttelton, which was built in 1853 and had to be demolished four years later — to become the leading architect of Canterbury Province. Canterbury College Great Hall, constructed of basalt and limestone and lined on its barrel-vaulted interior with kauri, rewarewa, tōtara and mataī, is a tour de force; it doesn't really matter that the original design's three towers were 'value managed' down to one. Mountfort's genius lies in his simultaneous adherence to the spirit of Gothic Revivalism and his relaxed observance of the rules of the genre. Note, for example, the arches above the windows of the Great Hall, which are segmented (gently curved) rather than lancet (pointed). The Great Hall retains a pointy Gothicness — the tower looks like a rocket about to be launched Godward — but also echoes a quality, 'not regularity of outline, but diversity', that Mountfort admired 'in Nature's buildings, the mountains and hills'.

Chemistry Laboratory

Collins and Harman, 1910
Historic Place Category 1

This attractive building illustrates the accommodating nature
of Gothic Revivalism when applied to an Oxbridge-inspired
campus setting. It could easily become less perpendicular and
more horizontal — see, for example, Cecil Wood's historicist
Hare Memorial Library at Christ College (pages 48–49) —
to better frame lawns or quadrangles. At the Chemistry
Laboratory a tower with an oriel window asymmetrically
divides a triple-height arrangement of mullioned windows
fitted between the building's buttresses; the tower has a
turret, the end buttresses have finials, and the roof has a
decorative ridge crest. A Gothic purist might find the design
eclectic, but the pre-Modernist architects of the early
twentieth century were not averse to stylistic promiscuity,
often favouring compositional effect over consistency. With
this building there is a strong sense of architects delighting
in the natural materials available to them in what was still
a relatively young colony. The Chemistry Laboratory is
testament to the state of the regional quarrying industry
in the early twentieth century: façade materials include
Halswell, Hoon Hay and Timaru basalt, and Ōamaru
limestone. Architects John James Collins (1855–1933)
and Richard Dacre Harman (1859–1927) had continued the
firm started by William Barnett Armson (1932/33–1883) in
1870. Collins and Harman were busy through the 37 years of
their partnership; their work included significant commercial
projects such as the Christchurch Press Building (1909,
demolished after the 2010–2011 earthquakes) and the still-
extant Sign of the Takahe roadhouse (1936) in the Port Hills,
as well as numerous gentry houses. Their connections helped.
Harman, in particular, got off to a flying, if competitive, start
in life as one of 15 children of prominent businessman and
politician Richard James Strachan Harman and his wife, Emma.

Richard Harman senior had studied at Rugby School under the famous headmaster Thomas Arnold. Richard Harman junior enthusiastically played the game named for the English school but was better at tennis, his long run as Canterbury singles champ only ended by future four-time Wimbledon champion Anthony Wilding (1883–1915). The Chemistry Laboratory was restored after the 2010–2011 earthquakes by Warren and Mahoney Architects (2017), and now houses the University of Canterbury's classics and music departments, back from their Ilam exile.

Chemistry Laboratory, The Arts Centre
Te Matatiki Toi Ora, Hereford Street.

Canterbury College Library (right), connected via
an arcade to the West Lecture Building (left).

Canterbury College Library

Collins and Harman, 1916
Historic Place Category 1

In 1913, 40 years after Benjamin Mountfort started designing buildings on the Canterbury College campus, the College received an architectural reboot. Samuel Hurst Seager (1855–1933), a member of the College's board of governors and a lecturer in its School of Fine Arts, produced a new master plan for the campus with a view to more explicitly realising Mountfort's Oxbridge intentions. The principal instrument of this ambition was a College library. For Seager, the College's lack of a dedicated library was a serious omission. 'In any complete College, the Library is the centre of the Intellectual part of College Life,' Seager wrote. 'This should be architecturally expressed by its occupying a prominent central position.' The insertion into the heart of the campus of a library, joined to neighbouring buildings by arcades at its east and west ends, also served a planning purpose by creating separate Oxbridge-style quadrangles to the north and south of the building.

The 1913 Student Carnival raised more than half of the £3500 cost of the building (less than $4 million in today's money, an impossibly inadequate figure for an equivalent contemporary building). Although Seager had produced the master plan, the commission for the library's design went to Collins and Harman, the official Canterbury College architects from around the early 1900s until the late 1920s. The basalt and limestone library complements earlier buildings on the campus, although some Gothic–Tudor fusion is evident in the building's extensive glazing and arched windows. Restored post-earthquakes, the building now houses a dealer art gallery.

Christ's College

Rolleston Avenue

The buildings around Christ's College quad constitute one of the strongest architectural compositions in New Zealand. The site's distinction is not a matter of fortunate happenstance: it was planned this way. From the start, the colonisers of Canterbury envisaged that an integral institution of the settlement would be a boys' school modelled on 'the great Grammar Schools of England'. As time went by, the aspirations of the school became, if anything, even grander, and Christ's took to taking its educational and cultural lead from the great 'public' schools of England. Christ's College was established on its present site adjacent to Hagley Park in 1856. Over the course of more than a century and a half, wealth, tradition and inter-generational fealty to the alma mater have found expression in the commission, preservation and careful augmentation of fine buildings by some of Christchurch's best architects, including the Mountforts (father and son), John Collins and Richard Harman, Cecil Wood, Paul Pascoe and Miles Warren.

A   Jacobs House

B   School House

C   Hare Memorial Library

D   Big School

E   Chapel

F   Harper and Julius Houses

G   Memorial Dining Room

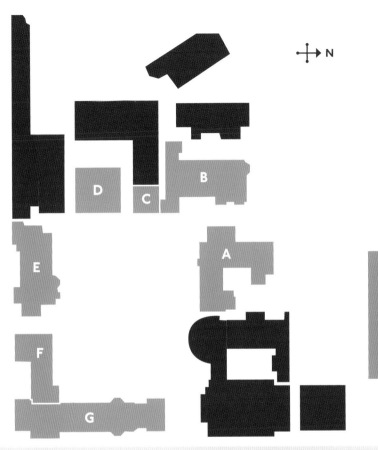

N

B

D

C

A

ROUTE 1–6

E

F

G

Rolleston Avenue

Gloucester Street

The Quadrangle at Christ's College,
Rolleston Avenue.

Jacobs House

Cecil Wood, 1930
Historic Place Category 2

Named for the first headmaster of Christ's College, Reverend Henry Jacobs (1824–1901), this boarding house on the north side of the quad was designed by Cecil Wood (1878–1947). It was Wood's third building on the College campus and was designed in formal and material sympathy to existing buildings on the quad, especially the neighbouring School House. On its quad side, the building is styled as an historicist blend of Gothic Revival and Collegiate Gothic, with an admixture of Georgian Revival to boot. This façade of the L-shaped, slate-roofed building is made of Hoon Hay rubble stone, relieved by the use of white Ōamaru stone on the entranceway, window surrounds and a string course, and red Redcliffs volcanic stone on the battlements. The string course is decorated with seven stone heads by local carver Frederick George Gurnsey (1868–1953). At the rear, the building is plainer, and presents an overtly neo-Georgian brick face to the Avon River.

School House

Cyril Mountfort; Armson, Collins and Harman, 1909
Historic Place Category 2

School House is a Collegiate Gothic building for boarders designed by Cyril Mountfort (1852–1920), and John James Collins (1855–1933) and Richard Dacre Harman (1859–1927). The main façade is constructed of local Halswell stone, with window arches in white Ōamaru stone, and features a small cloister. On its other, less visible sides, the building is brick. An observatory, designed by Cecil Wood, was added to the roof in 1936. Architecturally, School House could be seen as an act of filial piety; it is similar to the building that sits diagonally across the quad — Harper and Julius Houses (1886), designed by Cyril's father, Benjamin. Cyril Mountfort's career was overshadowed by his eminent father; John Collins and Richard Harman were more successful. Inheritors of the practice established in 1870 by William Barnett Armson, Collins and Harman worked in partnership for 37 years. (The firm itself lasted for 123 years.) Like Cyril Mountfort, Collins and Harman were old boys of Christ's College, and very clubbable — Harman was a prominent sportsman — and their social connections provided a steady stream of residential commissions from pastoral landowners and urban professionals. The story of Collins and Harman's progress is also a narrative of the changes in sensibility of an essentially conservative clientele, as local architectural tastes evolved from Gothic and Tudor Revival to Arts and Crafts and eventually modern bungalow.

Hare Memorial Library

Cecil Wood, 1915
Historic Place Category 1

With the design of Hare Memorial Library, Cecil Wood went a little wild — Hogwarts wild. The library, which was named for a long-serving chaplain and headmaster of Christ's College, was the first of Wood's three buildings around the quad. Gothic Revival had been established as the school's architectural style and stone as its building material. Wood demonstrated appropriate deference to precedent in the design of Hare Memorial Library, but introduced some Tudor twists in the form of an oriel window, arched gateway and chimneys, and half-timbering on the interior of the library, which was sited on the building's first floor. The Gothic gargoyles carved by Frederick Gurnsey look as if they have been captured in mid-leap from the building's stylistic apostasy. The variegated colour palette of the façade — grey Malvern stone, red Sumner volcanic stone and cream Mount Somers limestone — combine with Wood's antiquarian references to produce what is almost a parodically picturesque building. It is extraordinary to think, if you allow yourself to zoom out of the quad, spatially and temporally, that in 10 years' time Walter Gropius would be designing the Bauhaus building in Dessau, and a few years later Mies van der Rohe would have finished the Barcelona Pavilion.

Big School

**James Edward FitzGerald, 1863;
addition by Miles Warren, 1989**
Historic Place Category 1

Constructed of stone, with a slate roof, timber ceiling and
leaded windows, Big School was the first substantial building
on the Christ's College campus. It was designed in England,
with an eye to pedagogical tradition but little contextual
awareness — hence the roof pitched to counter alpine
snowfalls — by James Edward FitzGerald (1818–1896), one
of those energetic genre-busters with which Victorian Britain
abounded. FitzGerald started out as a junior in the Antiquities
Department of the British Museum, found quick promotion
and involved himself in social and political causes. As
Secretary of the Canterbury Association he helped plan the
Canterbury settlement and decided to emigrate to it, in short
order serving as a police sub-inspector, newspaper publisher
and farm owner. FitzGerald was elected superintendent of
Canterbury Province and was later a member of Parliament
with comparatively enlightened views on race relations.
Next, he became a Wellington senior civil servant before
heading a trade union for civil servants. In his spare time,
FitzGerald painted watercolours and wrote verse and drama;
his wife, Frances, presumably took primary responsibility
for the couple's 13 children. Big School seems to have been
the only building FitzGerald designed — he appears to have
been unfazed by his complete lack of architectural training. In
1989, the building received an addition of five gabled wings,
designed by an indubitably proper architect, Miles Warren.

Chapel

**Robert Speechly, 1867; additions by Benjamin
Mountfort (1883, 1887) and Paul Pascoe (1957)**
Historic Place Category 1

Christ's College Chapel was designed by Robert Speechly
(1840–1884), who came to Canterbury to supervise the
construction of ChristChurch Cathedral (see pages 104–05)
and function, effectively, as the Church of England's architect-
in-residence. Gothic Revivalism was the architectural
language of the mid-nineteenth-century Anglican Church,
and Speechly duly adopted the style for a modest stone
chapel that materially, and in the form of its steep slate roof,
complemented the existing Big School. Benjamin Mountfort
added transepts and a chancel (1883) and organ chamber
(1887) to the chapel, and that was it until Paul Pascoe (1908–
1976) designed a sympathetic extension to the south that
doubled the building's size. Pascoe was a Christ's College old
boy who trained with Cecil Wood before a sojourn in England
in the mid-1930s confirmed his Modernist inclinations.
(When it came to choosing its post-war architects, Christ's
College evidently did not let its traditionalism blind it to
design ability, especially, perhaps, if competence was allied
with alumnus status.) Pascoe was a highly regarded designer,
especially of houses and churches; airport architecture was
another of his specialties. After a decade in partnership with
Humphrey Hall (1912–1988), Pascoe was a sole practitioner
at the time he designed the extension to Christ's College
Chapel. Later, he formed another effective partnership with
Walter Linton (1927–2018).

Harper and Julius Houses

Benjamin Mountfort, 1886

Harper House and Julius House are day-boy houses, formerly called South Town and North Town — membership was determined by students' addresses in the city — that for nearly a century have occupied what was originally a classroom block, designed by Benjamin Mountfort, on the south side of the quad. Harper House was the first 'house' assigned to the Georgian Revival building; the bottom floor was converted to accommodate Julius House in 1931. Further renovations were undertaken in 1962 and 1981. After the building was damaged in the 2010–2011 earthquakes, it was seismically strengthened, and the exterior was restored under the supervision of Wilkie + Bruce Architects (2013). Christ's College is not short of atmospheric places that must imprint themselves forever in the memory of those who study there, but even amidst this evocative abundance the façade cloister of the Harper and Julius building is special. It is the sort of space boys love, an open-air den. On the day Patrick Reynolds took the photo at left, the cloister was in cricket-net mode, but right though the year it would be the best place on the quad to just hang out. The cloister has a sibling at School House, the quad-side building co-designed by Benjamin Mountfort's son, Cyril.

G

Memorial Dining Room

Cecil Wood, 1925
Historic Place Category 1

Christ's College Memorial Dining Room is probably, and deservedly, the most acclaimed work of Cecil Wood (1878–1947). The Dining Room memorialises old boys of the school who served in the First World War — over 130 lost their lives — and does so without stint: the Dining Room cost twice as much as the city's Bridge of Remembrance (see pages 70–71). Wood deployed the Collegiate Gothic style — species to the Gothic Revival genus — on a building that defines the east side of the quad and presents the school's public face to Rolleston Avenue. The building features a square tower where it meets Benjamin Mountfort's 1886 classroom block (Harper and Julius Houses), half a dozen buttresses on the east and west sides, oriel bay windows and a façade composed of grey Hoon Hay rubble, Redcliffs volcanic stone and Ōamaru limestone. Inside, Wood got medieval; historian Ruth Helms has pointed out the Dining Room's links to the Great Hall at the Oxford college Christ Church, especially in the use of timber linenfold panelling — timber, that is, carved in vertical folds — and ribbed hammerbeam Oregon roof trusses, their ends decorated with winged figures carved by Frederick Gurnsey. At one end of the hall, which can accommodate 350 diners, there is a raised dais; at the other end, a musicians' gallery. The addition (1988) at the north end of the building, housing school offices, was designed by Miles Warren.

Cathedral Grammar Junior School

2 Chester Street

Andrew Barrie Lab and Tezuka Architects, 2016

Andrew Barrie is that rare figure in New Zealand architecture: a full-time academic who also practises. Barrie teaches at the University of Auckland School of Architecture and Planning, where he is a professor, and carries out his design work under the auspices of his studio, Andrew Barrie Lab. He is, as well, one of New Zealand's most prolific architectural writers, and his curatorial work includes exhibitions at the Venice Architecture Biennale. After completing his doctoral studies in Tokyo, Barrie worked in the office of the eminent architect Toyo Ito. He has maintained his Japanese connections and teamed up with Takaharu and Yui Tezuka of Tezuka Architects to design the junior school (years 1–3) for the Anglican Cathedral Grammar School. Tezuka Architects received international acclaim — and the attention of Cathedral Grammar School — for their Fuji Kindergarten (Tokyo, 2007), which features a large oval roof deck on which children can play and run. A roof deck is incorporated into Cathedral Grammar Junior School, which was conceived as a 'garden school' with an internal layout allowing for both discrete and open-plan teaching spaces. The building's structural design draws on Barrie's research into innovative timber construction materials and technologies. Laminated veneer lumber (LVL) posts and beams slot precisely together after being cut with computer numerical control (CNC) machines to a tolerance of half a millimetre over 12 metres.

ROUTE 2: WEST BANK

This city pocket bordered on three sides by the Avon River–Ōtākaro includes two very different memorial sites, one commemorating those who fell in the First World War, and the other those who died in the earthquake of 22 February 2011. Also in this part of the city are the two Christchurch public art galleries, designed 40 years apart, and two significant examples of local concrete Modernism: the early 1980s brute that has been converted to house council offices, and the engaging 1960s building which Miles Warren, the leading Christchurch architect of his generation, designed as his practice office and town house.

Te Hononga Christchurch Civic Building

53 Hereford Street

**Government Architect's Office, MoW, 1981;
Athfield Architects, 2010**

Te Hononga Christchurch Civic Building impressively
represents several phenomena of both architectural and
social significance. It is a case study in sustainability and —
literally — a monument to the role of the state as architect
and builder in New Zealand and to the historic importance
of the post office in the socio-economic life of the country.
The building was designed as a mail sorting facility by the
Architectural Division (headed by the Government Architect)
of the Ministry of Works and Development (MoW). It started
its project life in 1965, but MoW jobs had a long lead time
and the building was not completed until 1981. The grunty
industrial building expressed the MoW's Brutalist tendencies
of the 1960s and '70s and a concomitant partiality for
reinforced concrete as a construction medium. (In an era
of import restrictions, concrete offered the advantage of
high local content.) The post office's enfeeblement after
the economic deregulation of the late 1980s eventually
robbed the building of its purpose, and in the first decade
of this century it was converted by Athfield Architects into
the headquarters of Christchurch City Council. The energy
embodied in the building's construction has not been wasted,
nor has the structure been much changed. Concrete façade
panels were replaced with glass to admit light into the
building's seven 5.8-metre-high floors, and a ground-level
walkway now connects the business entrance on Hereford
Street with the public entrance on Gloucester Street.

West Avon Flats

279 Montreal Street

Wilfred Melville Lawry, 1936
Historic Place Category 2

Art Deco? You cannot be serious! Rarely has there been such an instance of a design style serving itself up so heedlessly to the judgement of the future. Captivated by surface and smitten with glamour, Art Deco was fashionable for a couple of decades — a frivolous filling sandwiched between two world wars. Its architectural crime, in the eyes of later critics, was to be modern without being Modernist, to be too gratuitous in its ornamentalism. (Art Deco architects might have argued they were just putting the fun into function.) But that is exactly why the style had its moment, and why, even today, in a popularity contest between, say, great New York skyscrapers, the Chrysler Building (William Van Alen, 1930), with its gleaming sunburst spire, would win hands down over the austerely elegant Seagram Building (Mies van der Rohe, 1958). Art Deco spread around the world, reaching into New Zealand suburbia and more impressively into downtown Napier after the 1931 earthquake. The West Avon Flats were designed in the relatively restrained Moderne variant of the genre by Wilfred Melville Lawry (1894–1980), a Deco specialist, and First World War veteran and Methodist church organist. Lawry's design, downscaled from six storeys and 36 flats to two storeys and eight flats, was realised, reassuringly, at a time of heightened seismic consciousness, in reinforced concrete.

65 Cambridge Terrace

Warren and Mahoney, 1962 (with additions up to 1989)

In 1955, Miles Warren returned to Christchurch after two
years in England experiencing, as an architect for London
County Council, the heyday of UK municipal Modernism
and springtime of New Brutalism. Back home, he launched
a practice which was soon joined by Maurice Mahoney (1929–
2018) — for 35 years, Dr Watson to Warren's Sherlock Holmes
— and embarked on one of the hottest streaks in New Zealand
architecture. For a decade and a half, the hits kept coming:
Dorset Street Flats (1957), Harewood Crematorium Chapel
(1963), College House (1964), Christchurch College Chapel
and Library (1967–1970), Christchurch Town Hall (1972).
Even among these peers, 65 Cambridge Terrace is
outstanding. Sited in what was then a residential zone, the
building was cannily conceived as both an office for Warren
and Mahoney and a regulation-satisfying house. It is a
miniaturist masterpiece, real architect's architecture, but also
a builder's building. 'Miles made a great play of how he put
his buildings together,' wrote the architect and critic David
Mitchell, 'articulating every joint, which is a fabricator's way
of looking at architecture.' At 65 Cambridge Terrace Warren
was showing off, literally, treating the town to a Brutalist
exposition of concrete beams and blocks, but also exhibiting
an extremely deft command of details and a typically impish
capacity to delight.

Oi Manawa Canterbury Earthquake National Memorial

Avon River at Montreal and Oxford Streets

Grega Vezjak, 2017

Oi Manawa Canterbury Earthquake National Memorial opened on 22 February 2017, the sixth anniversary of the earthquake that killed 185 people in Christchurch. The memorial encompasses both banks on a curve of the Avon River downstream from the Montreal Street bridge. Along the south bank of the hectare-sized site, a riverside walkway leads past a 111-metre-long, 3.6-metre-high Carrara marble wall bearing the names of those who lost their lives; the north bank is an informal reserve that offers contemplative views across the river to the memorial wall. The memorial is the result of a design competition that attracted 339 entries from around the world and was won by Slovenian architect Grega Vezjak. Not surprisingly, Vezjak's design has an affinity with the most influential memorial of the past half-century, Maya Lin's Vietnam Veterans Memorial (1982) in Washington DC. Where Lin's memorial wall is partially buried in the earth, Vezjak's wall sinks below street level to connect with the Avon River. Oi Manawa — 'the tremor or quivering of the heart' — is the sort of memorial that bereaved families indicated they wanted: not an object or a ruin, but a place, close to nature. A visit to W. H. Gummer's memorial arch at the Bridge of Remembrance (1924), a short distance away (see pages 70–71), serves to show how far official remembering has come in the last hundred years.

Bridge of Remembrance

Avon River at Cashel Street

Gummer and Prouse, 1924
Historic Place Category 1

In the years after the First World War, in which around
18,000 New Zealanders lost their lives, hundreds of
memorials were erected around the country. Memorial
architecture included statues, obelisks, towers, gates and
even entire buildings, such as Auckland's War Memorial
Museum. The Bridge of Remembrance is one of the two
main Christchurch war memorials, the other being the
Citizens' War Memorial in Cathedral Square (currently out
of bounds). Confusingly, the Bridge of Remembrance is a
title that covers both the bridge over the Avon River built
in 1873 by engineer Edward George Wright (1831–1902)
and the memorial arch at the bridge's east end, designed by
William Henry Gummer (1884–1966). Steeped in Beaux-
Arts classicism, gifted and prolific, Gummer is one of the
outstanding figures in New Zealand architecture. Before
the First World War, he worked in London for Edwin Lutyens
(1869–1944), the pre-eminent British architect of his time.
Gummer's arch, made of concrete faced with Tasmanian
stone, could keep easy company with structures from
Lutyens' extensive post-war votive catalogue, such as the
Cenotaph in Whitehall (1920) and the Arch of Remembrance
in Leicester (1925). The Christchurch arch's connection
to the British Empire's war memorial design language is
strengthened by the incorporation of decorative elements
— wreaths, laurels and lions — by the noted Christchurch
carver Frederick George Gurnsey (1868–1953).

151 Cambridge Terrace

Jasmax, 2014

While the 2011 Christchurch earthquake was immediately frightening, for people who grew up in the city the long-running aftermath has been profoundly disorienting. As damaged or vulnerable buildings were demolished all around the CBD, the concept of place was also dismantled. In parts of the central city, there was no 'there' there anymore. Which brings us to the subject of context in architecture: when architects discuss the factors that have influenced their designs, they habitually invoke the notion of 'context'. The reference may be meaningful or moonshine, dutiful or desperate; it can allude to neighbouring buildings or the wider city, local architectural history or a building type, cultural tropes or features of the natural world. The latter well of inspiration was the one visited by Jasmax when designing this large commercial building on a prominent site near the Avon River. Absent any other contextual clues in what had become a demolition zone, the architects turned to the river itself and echoed the Avon's winding course in the aqua-coloured glass façade of the new building. The building was an early indicator of a generic shift in post-quake Christchurch from masonry buildings — heavy but seismically weak — to more resilient, often extensively glazed structures of sudden contemporaneity.

Toi Moroki Centre of Contemporary Art (CoCA) Gallery

66 Gloucester Street

Minson, Henning-Hansen and Dines, 1968

It's not easy to appreciate, from the perspective of the present, how radical some buildings from the past must have appeared when they were new. Take, for example, Toi Moroki Centre of Contemporary Art (CoCA) Gallery. Built by what was then the Canterbury Society of Arts to replace its former premises — two late nineteenth-century brick buildings on another site, one of them designed by, yes, Benjamin Mountfort — CoCA introduced itself to its heritage neighbourhood with uncompromising severity. Even in a city softened up to concrete Modernism by a decade of Miles Warren Brutalism, the building, with its façade of twin aggregate slabs, must have come as a shock. How did it happen? Because the client was a private entity, and therefore not subject to the committee caution that can cripple public projects in New Zealand, and because the panel that wrote the brief included three architects — Miles Warren, Peter Beaven and Paul Pascoe. And, especially, because the commission went to one of the able Modernist practices that characterised Christchurch architecture in the 1960s, the partnership of Stewart William Minson (1904–2006), Holger Henning-Hansen (1921–1996) and John Rayner Dines (1927–1993). This fine building seems particularly congruent with the Scandinavian Modernist inclinations of Danish immigrant Henning-Hansen. If you look up, it is possible to discern, in CoCA's rooftop cluster of pyramidal skylights, a reference to the Christchurch tradition of pointy architecture.

Christchurch Art Gallery Te Puna o Waiwhetū

Corner Worcester Boulevard and Montreal Street

The Buchan Group, 2003

In 1998, Christchurch Council staged a design competition for a public art gallery to replace the small Robert McDougall Art Gallery (Edward Armstrong, 1932) located in the Botanic Gardens. (That building is extant but closed for repair.) The new building was to occupy a new site, close to the city's two strongest collections of heritage buildings, The Arts Centre and Christ's College. (No pressure, then.) To some local surprise, the competition, which attracted 94 entries, was won by the Auckland office of a practice of Australian origin, The Buchan Group. The competition judges were impressed by the most obvious feature of the design, the glass façade on the west elevation. With its 'association with the curved shapes of the Koru and to the serpentine course of the Avon River,' the judges said, the glazed wall expresses 'the public face of the building, its identity as an Art Gallery.' The latter remark was revealing: formal excitement had come to be regarded as an essential quality of the art museum. The Guggenheim had worked its effect, first in New York (Frank Lloyd Wright, 1959) and then, even more influentially, in Bilbao (Frank Gehry, 1997). However, the glass wall is not just a signifier; it serves to connect the building to an extensive sculpture garden and admits light into the three-storey lobby that fronts the traditional boxes that exhibit the gallery's excellent collection.

ROUTE 3:
EAST BANK

A range of the types of architectural projects
undertaken in the centre of Christchurch
during the city's post-earthquake recovery
can be seen in the streets on the east side of
the river. There are old buildings that have
been, or are being, restored; new commercial
and institutional buildings; and two of the
important civic 'anchor' projects that have
served to underwrite the rebuilding of
the city. The latter adjacent buildings, one
a bus station (Hine-Pāka) and the other a
juridical and emergency services complex
(Te Omeka), demonstrate contemporary
official attitudes to public architecture, and
the recent commitment to acknowledge the
Māori presence in Ōtautahi-Christchurch.

Church of St Michael and All Angels, and Belfry

84 Oxford Terrace

William Fitzjohn Crisp, 1872 (church);
Benjamin Mountfort, 1861 (belfry)
Historic Place Category 1

In 1851, the Anglican settlers of Christchurch built the first church on the Canterbury Plains, initially called Christ Church, then re-named St Michael and All Angels. The congregation soon outgrew the church and commissioned a replacement on the same site from William Fitzjohn Crisp (1846–1924), a young English immigrant architect. Crisp designed the building in the Gothic Revival style then popular in British ecclesiastical architecture. There was one significant concession to local circumstances: a meeting of the parishioners, reported Christchurch newspaper *The Star* in December 1869, concluded that 'owing to the late severe shocks of earthquake . . . it would be useless to attempt building any part of stone. Therefore it was decided that wood should be the material.' Matai was the native timber chosen for the structure — supported by a rubble stone foundation — and the combination of this dark wood and English stained glass windows makes for a richly atmospheric interior. The relationship between the clients and their architect broke down during construction and Crisp returned to Britain in 1871. Frederick Strouts (1834–1919), a noted designer of houses for the Canterbury gentry, was appointed supervising architect in his place. The church never received its planned bell tower and spire but is kept company by the belfry from the original church, designed by the inevitable Benjamin Mountfort (1825–1898).

Ao Tawhiti Building

5 Mollett Street

Stephenson & Turner, 2019

All schools have 'character', but some schools proclaim their particularity more overtly than others. In Christchurch, the city's oldest school, Christ's College, is the archetype of the traditional 'character' school, its identity expressed through archaic uniforms, arcane rituals and 170 years of careful stewardship of its architectural stock. This is character by accretion, but character can also be a matter of contrivance. Christchurch's newest school, Ao Tawhiti — in longform, Ao Tawhiti Unlimited Discovery — is a 'designated character school'. This type of school belongs to the state education system but has considerable discretion in pursuing its own course, which in Ao Tawhiti's case is 'self-directed learning'. Ao Tawhiti, which combines primary and secondary school students in one big building, is resolutely a central-city school and a welcome presence in the slow-to-develop 'South Frame' of the city's post-earthquake urban blueprint. Ao Tawhiti doesn't have any grounds; instead, it treats the city as its campus by piggybacking on civic amenities such as parks and libraries. The building is a pronounced example of the contemporary blurring of educational and commercial architecture. A steel and concrete structure, with a façade of terracotta tiles and irregular fenestration, surrounds a central atrium that connects four floors of flexible spaces. The building was designed by Stephenson & Turner, an architectural and engineering practice of Australian origin that came to New Zealand in 1956. The company no longer exists in Australia, but in New Zealand it continues to add to an extensive portfolio of commercial and institutional projects.

ROUTE 3-17

Environment Canterbury Building

200 Tuam Street

Wilson & Hill Architects, 2016

Environment Canterbury, often shortened to the even hipper term ECan, is the brand name of Canterbury Regional Council, which has responsibility for many aspects of land and water use in the largest of New Zealand's administrative regions. Regional councils may have far less discretion than their Provincial Government forebears enjoyed in their nineteenth-century heyday, but they still have significant clout. Environment Canterbury, for example, has jurisdiction of all the river catchments in a 4-million-hectare area that stretches for 400 kilometres from the Clarence River in the north to the Waitaki River in the south. That puts the elected body at the centre of the water politics of a farming area that has undergone rapid, and very thirsty, intensification in the last 20 years. For Environment Canterbury, the second decade of the twenty-first century was a tough time. In 2010, the National government used policy differences among elected councillors as the *casus belli* to dismiss councillors and replace them with unelected commissioners — a fully elected council was not returned to office until 2019 — and in the 2010–2011 earthquakes Environment Canterbury's premises were badly damaged. The organisation's new building, designed by Wilson & Hill Architects, is an exemplar of post-quake architecture. The five-storey building, which accommodates 450 staff, rests on piles driven 16 metres into the ground and employs base isolation and superstructural flexibility to provide earthquake resistance. Resistance to political interference? That's another story.

Post and Telegraph Office

185 High Street

John Thomas Mair, 1932

If you prefer Art Deco in its vertical version, rather than its horizontal form as expressed by the West Avon Flats (see pages 64–65), the former Post and Telegraph Office on the corner of High and Tuam Streets is a building for you. It looks good these days, having been restored, strengthened and adapted to house a cinema and café by owners who bought it from the government when the state sold off its assets in the 1980s. The building was designed by John Thomas (J. T.) Mair (1876–1959), who served as Government Architect from 1923 to 1941, a period in which concrete and steel were replacing brick and timber in larger-scale New Zealand architecture and Modernism was receiving a cautious welcome. Dexterous in his craft and diligent in character, Mair designed post offices and courthouses up and down the country, and such fine landmark buildings as the Spanish Mission-style Blue Baths in Rotorua (1929), and the Moderne-style Stout Street Departmental Building in Wellington (1937) and Jean Batten Place Departmental Building in Auckland (1942). Mair, who was born in Invercargill, studied architecture at the University of Pennsylvania (1906–1908). Before returning to New Zealand, he topped up his education with a tour of Classical and Romanesque European architecture, an experience that may have informed his unironic deployment of pilasters and festoons on the façade of the Post and Telegraph Office.

Stranges and Glendenning Hill Building

Corner High and Lichfield Streets

Sheppard & Rout Architects, 2014

At the turn of the twentieth century, the corner where High Street meets Lichfield Street as it cuts diagonally across the city grid was the busiest intersection in Christchurch. The site was occupied by the thriving department store — then New Zealand's largest — of Strange and Company. William Strange (1832–1914) was an immigrant draper whose retail business eventually employed 600 people; he also owned a factory and, for a decade, a 10,000-acre farm on the Selwyn River. On the sides of the V where High Street and Lichfield Street met, Strange had commissioned, from the leading Christchurch architecture practice founded by William Barnett Armson (1832/33–1883), a series of Italianate buildings, culminating in the four-storey block clad in Ōamaru stone that sat at the apex of the triangular site. After Strange's death, his company slowly foundered, and this latter building became one of many Christchurch heritage buildings whose architectural merit was unrewarded by profitable use. When the Strange's building was ruined by the 2010 and 2011 earthquakes it was replaced, in a spectacular deposition of stone by steel and glass, with a building designed by Sheppard & Rout Architects and seismically engineered to 180 per cent of the building code. In a small-scale way, the building internalises the old bustle of the High Street / Lichfield Street corner through the incorporation of laneways — a popular contemporary urban design trope — that lead to a sheltered courtyard served by cafés and bars.

Te Omeka Justice and Emergency Services Precinct

20 Lichfield Street

Warren and Mahoney Architects,
Cox Architecture, Opus Architecture, 2017

The Christchurch Justice and Emergency Services Precinct was an 'anchor' project in the city's post-2011 reconstruction. Designed by Warren and Mahoney Architects, with Australian prison and police station specialist Cox Architecture and New Zealand infrastructure consultants Opus Architecture, the three-building precinct combines juridical institutions and emergency services — courts, police, corrections, fire and ambulance services — in a 42,000-square-metre complex occupying a city block and surrounding a central courtyard. The administrative centralisation facilitated by the precinct is a post-earthquake strategy to strengthen civic resilience, but the project was also an opportunity to design spaces that suit and signal contemporary function. This modernising impulse is most evident in the treatment of the law courts. In contrast to the former Christchurch Law Courts (see pages 128–29), with its convoluted organisation of cramped courts and offices, the new courts building is arranged more generously and transparently around an atrium with views out to the city and the Port Hills. The precinct is a behemoth with a butch façade — a jutting display of concrete and glass boxes — but a more sensitive interior. 'It's light and airy,' admitted one local judge, before putting on his black cap to add, 'but I wanted dark and scary.' More profoundly, a higher-ranked judge expressed his opposition to the Justice Precinct's disregard for the principle that the courts and the police are arms of government that are, and must be seen to be, separate.

Hine-Pāka Christchurch Bus Interchange

Corner Lichfield and Colombo Streets

Architectus, 2015

While railway stations in New Zealand's big cities were monuments that declared a pride in their purpose, bus stations have commonly expressed nothing but civic parsimony. In large part, the difference was down to the calendar of the country's development. A century ago, the railway connected the nation; train travel was significant, and a city's train station was both primary portal and status symbol. Buses, when they came along, decades later, were just another transport mode, serving car-less urban commuters and less affluent inter-city travellers. Bus stations, where they existed, were desultory waiting or loitering areas from which cold draughts never managed to dispel foul air. This history explains why the Hine-Pāka Christchurch Bus Interchange is such a welcome surprise. The building — and thank goodness its lifeless English title has been animated by the name of a Ngāi Tahu ancestor — was the first Christchurch post-earthquake anchor project and it set a reassuring precedent for new public architecture in the city. Designed by Architectus, a practice of Auckland origins with a strong portfolio of Christchurch buildings (see also pages 120–21 and 154–55), the bus station is an L-shaped building that wraps around a prominent city corner to provide comfortable shelter — underfloor heating! natural light! clean toilets! — and easy access to bus platforms. The dramatic folded roof provides generous internal volume and signals the building's presence, and is also a hat-tip to the local Gothic tradition.

The Terrace

Oxford Terrace

Jasmax and NH Architecture, 2018

In the decade before the 2011 Christchurch earthquake, Oxford Terrace between Hereford and Cashel Streets became known as 'The Strip', a block of bars and restaurants with an atmosphere often described, rather euphemistically, as 'lively'. The row of century-old buildings facing the Avon River was badly damaged in the 2011 earthquake but, at a time when many hospitality businesses were fleeing the central city, the landowner opted to redevelop and rebrand The Strip. Now, it is 'The Terrace', a suite of mixed-use commercial buildings designed by Jasmax and Australian firm NH Architecture. The buildings are individual expressions of a site planning model. Rather than being arranged as a line of joined-up buildings, The Terrace is a complex of buildings organised around laneways that, as architects say, 'activate' the interior of the site. 'Porosity' is the principle in play: pedestrian throughways multiply the number of street-level commercial frontages. Melbourne's successful opening-up of its CBD laneways to hospitality use is the precedent being followed at The Terrace. As for the buildings themselves, they look different, being distinguished by the shape of their forms and the materials of their façades, but they act the same. What they have in common, and what will declare their vintage as surely as Gothic pointed arches or Brutalist concrete beams, are the cantilevered balconies and expanses of glazing offering prospects of the Avon.

77 Hereford Street

Warren and Mahoney Architects, 1981

The office building at 77 Hereford Street marks the end of the mid-career stage of the partnership of the influential architecture practice led by Miles Warren and Maurice Mahoney (1929–2018). From the late 1960s Warren and Mahoney had scaled up as the firm began to receive commissions commensurate with its ambition. Christchurch Town Hall (1972) and the New Zealand Chancery building in Washington DC (1979) were the most prestigious projects of this consolidation phase, but at the same time that Warren and Mahoney was producing these bespoke creations the practice was also designing a diffusion range of Modernist buildings that significantly raised the bar for commercial architecture in Christchurch. The series of seven- to eight-storey, pre-cast concrete office buildings starting with the SIMU Building (1966, demolished after the 2011 earthquake) and culminating in 77 Hereford Street (originally the General Accident Building, 1981) typify Warren and Mahoney's middle years, just as the lineage of small in-situ concrete and concrete block houses and flats characterised the practice's youth. What made these office buildings appealing — and what continues to distinguish 77 Hereford Street in an increasingly thin-skinned city — was the chiaroscuro effect of a rhythmic repetition of deeply recessed windows. There was a functional reason for this façade form: it offered protective shading to a building without air-conditioning, while also providing occupants with natural light and views.

Municipal Chambers — Our City Ōtautahi

159 Oxford Terrace and Worcester Boulevard

Samuel Hurst Seager, 1887
Historic Place Category 1

If Christchurch architecture is a relay — and a respect for lineage is a characteristic of the city — then Samuel Hurst Seager (1855–1933) would be first baton change. Benjamin Mountfort (1825–1898) employed Seager; Seager hired Cecil Wood (1878–1947); Wood employed Miles Warren (1929–). This is a very strong line-up, and Seager, as a pivotal figure in New Zealand architecture, certainly justifies his place. Seager started on 'the tools' in his father's building company. He built the first Canterbury College buildings for Mountfort, then worked for the architect before studying in England. On his return to Christchurch he announced his presence by winning the 1885 competition to design the city's Municipal Chambers. Seager's competition entry, portentously titled 'Design with Beauty: Build with Truth' — the phrase is the motto of his alma mater, London's Architecture Association — was in the decorative and eclectic Queen Anne style that was enjoying a comeback in Britain. The design featured four differentiated façades and incorporated the figures of 'Industry' and 'Concord', early works by English sculptor George Frampton (1860–1928). It was all too much for some Christchurch critics, and Mountfort had to vouch for the building. Seager went on to design gentry homes, model workers' houses and overseas war memorials; he wrote, taught, and promoted town planning and professional standards. The repair of the earthquake-damaged Municipal Chambers would be a tribute to his legacy.

Worcester Chambers

69 Worcester Boulevard

Cecil Wood, 1928
Historic Place Category 2

Looking at old buildings can be like reading old novels.
The florid expressions and rhetorical flourishes that
characterised pre-Modernist literature have their equivalents
in pre-Modernist architecture, and the diet can be too
rich for contemporary taste. But one historical style that
is easier to digest is Georgian architecture, which valued
symmetry, proportion and a certain material frugality above
flamboyant forms and box-of-tricks ornamentation. The
Georgian style enjoyed a revival in Anglo-Saxon countries
in the early twentieth century and in Christchurch was
championed by Cecil Wood (1878–1947). The building
now known as Worcester Chambers is a nice little example
of Wood's Georgian Revival phase. Designed to house the
Digby family's commercial school (curriculum: shorthand,
typing, book-keeping, etc.), the brick building has a hipped
slate roof with — a little indulgently — two cornice-topping
urns, double-hung sash windows, cement quoins at either
end of the street elevation and a scalloped cement band
at footpath level. Wood could probably have designed
this building in his sleep, not that he would have, being
by all accounts a person of much integrity. Historian Ruth
Helms suggests Wood deserves a place in the front rank of
New Zealand inter-war architecture alongside Auckland's
W. H. Gummer (1884–1966) and Wellington's William
Gray Young (1895–1962). In his later career, Wood's
traditionalist inclinations attracted some Modernist
disdain, even if his talent continued to be acknowledged.

ROUTE 4: OLD CENTRE

The most visible reminder of the destruction of the 2010–2011 earthquakes is the ruined ChristChurch Cathedral, the focal point of Christchurch's historic city centre. While the debate about the Cathedral raged, other damaged buildings were restored, and new buildings — including the celebrated 'Cardboard' Cathedral — appeared in the precinct comprising Cathedral Square and the second Christchurch square to be named after a Protestant martyr, in this case Hugh Latimer. This route also takes in some of the the city's more important cultural and social sites: Tūranga (the new Christchurch Central Library); the Isaac Theatre Royal; and Tākaro ā Poi, the Margaret Mahy Playground.

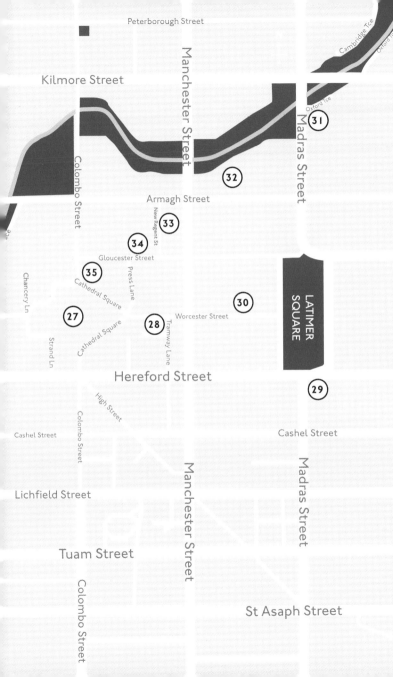

Peterborough Street

Kilmore Street

Manchester Street

Cambridge Tce

Oxford Tce

Oxford Tce

Colombo Street

Madras Street

(31)

(32)

Armagh Street

New Regent St

(33)

(34)

Gloucester Street

Press Lane

Chancery Ln

(35)

Cathedral Square

(27)

(30)

LATIMER
SQUARE

Cathedral Square

(28)

Worcester Street

Strand Ln

Tramway Lane

Hereford Street

(29)

Cashel Street

High Street

Colombo Street

Cashel Street

Cashel Street

Lichfield Street

Manchester Street

Madras Street

Tuam Street

Colombo Street

St Asaph Street

ChristChurch Cathedral

Cathedral Square

George Gilbert Scott, Benjamin Mountfort, 1864–1904
Historic Place Category 1

ChristChurch Cathedral has long enjoyed the status of civic symbol, but latterly it attracted a different sort of attention as the focus of the post-earthquake debate about heritage preservation. Actually, 'debate' is too tame a term for the vitriolic exchange of opinions, between savers and scrappers, about the fate of the badly damaged Church of England cathedral. (A complete account of this episode would require a Trollopian grasp of feline ecclesiastical politics.) The building reduced to rubble in the 2011 earthquake was designed by the English Gothic Revival architect George Gilbert Scott (1811–1878), with considerable later input by Benjamin Mountfort (1825–1898). Scott's original design for the cathedral — the epicentre of Anglicanism in New Zealand's most Anglican city — was for a cost-sensitive and earthquake-resistant timber church, but the Bishop of Christchurch wanted a stone building. On-site supervision of construction, which began in 1864, was carried out by Robert Speechly (1840–1884) and, following his departure from Christchurch in 1868, by Benjamin Mountfort. Over the years, Mountfort made changes to Scott's design — on the exterior, where he substituted stone for timber in the spire, and especially in the interior, where he designed much of the furniture and a number of stained glass windows. When Mountfort died in 1898, his son Cyril (1852–1920) saw the project through to its 1904 conclusion. In 2017, after a litigious interlude, the local Anglican synod resolved to restore, not replace, the cathedral. The statue of John Robert Godley (1814–1861), 'The Founder of Canterbury', presumably will retain its privileged position in Cathedral Square.

Old Government Building

28 Cathedral Square and Worcester Street

Joseph Clarkson Madison, 1913
Historic Place Category 1

The Government Building — sometimes referred to in
the plural — was commissioned by the pro-public works
Liberal government led by Sir Joseph Ward (1856–1930)
to house the Christchurch offices of central government
departments. For some reason, the design job did not go to
the Government Architect, Edwardian Baroque aficionado
John Campbell (1857–1942). Instead, local architect Joseph
Clarkson Madison (1850–1923) was chosen, perhaps
because he possessed big-building experience — hotels
and freezing works were his specialties — or perhaps some
design devolution was deemed politic. However Madison
won the project, he certainly seems to have relished his
opportunity. Madison, who knew how to dress up a big box,
gave the Government Building the full Italian Renaissance
Palazzo treatment: rusticated stone base; two-levels of
brick façade punctuated symmetrically by tall windows in
highly articulated frames; Corinthian entabulature and a
parapet (now replaced in replica). There's a lot going on, but
the standout — literally — features of the building are the
columns surmounting the north entrance and, especially, the
extraordinary four-columned recessed portico (or *portico in
antis*) above the west entrance. The building was occupied by
government departments for 70 years until it was abandoned
during the state asset-shedding of the late 1980s. It was
threatened with demolition until the city council bought
it and then sold it to developers. In its restored state, the
building functions as a hotel.

'Cardboard' Cathedral

234 Hereford Street

Shigeru Ban, with Warren and Mahoney Architects, 2013

The genesis of the Christchurch Transitional or 'Cardboard' Cathedral was so serendipitous that the theistically inclined might call it miraculous. Shortly after the February 2011 earthquake wrecked ChristChurch Cathedral, local Anglican cleric Craig Dixon came across an article about the Japanese architect Shigeru Ban, famous for his design of emergency structures, and then contacted Ban asking what he would charge to design a temporary cathedral in Christchurch. And so it came to pass that Christchurch now has the only building in New Zealand designed — for no fee — by a winner of international architecture's top personal award, the Pritzker Prize. Of course, the story of the building's realisation was not quite so straightforward, but the project was characterised throughout by goodwill and collegiality, qualities notably absent from the debate about the fate of the 'real' Anglican cathedral. The article that caught Reverend Dixon's attention focused on a temporary church, made of paper tubes, that Ban had designed in Kobe after the 1995 Great Hanshin earthquake. Ban proposed a similar, although larger, building for Christchurch, but modified the structural design to accommodate local manufacturing capabilities and the church's escalation of the projected life of the 'temporary' 700-seat cathedral from 10 to 50 years. This is a deceptively sophisticated building. The structure's 98 six-metre-long cardboard tubes are reinforced by timber beams and steel bracing. Up top, a polycarbonate roof twists into hyperbolic paraboloids; underneath, a 900-millimetre concrete raft protects against ground liquefaction. Forty-nine translucent coloured panels designed by Ban and his colleague Yoshie Narimatsu illuminate the dramatic, triangular main façade.

Christchurch Club

154 Worcester Street

Benjamin Mountfort, 1862
Historic Place Category 1

Scarcely had British settlers arrived in Canterbury than they set about creating institutions that would make them feel at home. For a group of wealthy landowners, a gentlemen's club was high on the social agenda. The Christchurch Club would be a city base for the country gentry, a place where business and politics could be transacted — homogeneously, in both a class and a gender sense. (Dissident professional and business members soon started their own club — the Canterbury Club.) Benjamin Mountfort was appointed to design the Christchurch Club's building, and produced an Italian Villa arrangement of a central tower flanked by two wings. Mountfort historian Ian Lochhead speculates that the use of this style, popular with bourgeois clients in Britain from around 1840 and later in Australasia and America, may have been a compromise between Mountfort's Gothic Revival inclinations and club members' preference for the more formal Italian Palazzo style associated with gentlemen's clubs in London. Another historian, Melanie Lovell-Smith, notes, drily, that the perception of the Italian Villa style as 'comparatively informal and as both elegant yet rural' made it 'a suitable combination for a club basing itself on English upper-class institutions but establishing itself in the middle of what was still a swamp'. Damaged in the 2011 earthquake, the building was restored by Warren and Mahoney Architects.

Oxford Terrace Baptist Church

288 Oxford Terrace

Andrew Barrie Lab, 2017

In the late 1870s, Christchurch Baptists got themselves sufficiently organised to build a substantial church. Not surprisingly, the design did not conform to the Gothic Revivalism that had become the house style of an Anglican city. Instead, the Baptists went Classical; E. J. Sanders, an architect of elusive biography, designed a brick building fronted with a pediment-and-columns portico. The church, which opened in 1881, was not peculiar in its design dissent: a denominational precedent had been set by the Classical Baptist Metropolitan Tabernacle in London (William Willmer Pocock, 1861), and Auckland's Baptist Tabernacle (Edmund Bell, 1885) was also treated to a portico inspired by the Pantheon in Rome. (There is some irony in the Baptists rejecting the architectural tradition of the Church of England only to embrace that of Rome.) In the 2011 earthquake, the Oxford Terrace Baptist Church suffered a spectacular structural collapse. This event forced church authorities to take stock. It's not cynical to suggest that for many Christchurch congregations, which had struggled over recent decades to reconcile heritage architecture and contemporary ecclesiastical practices, the earthquake was a God-given opportunity. The Baptists now have a modern church of understated form and flexible function designed by Andrew Barrie. Materials from the Modernist palette — concrete, timber and steel — that has served Christchurch well are deployed to appropriately austere effect. History gets a nod in a little parade of columns salvaged from the ruins of the original church.

Tākaro ā Poi Margaret Mahy Family Playground

Avon River at Manchester Street

Opus International Consultants, with Boffa Miskell, LandLAB, Tina Dyer, Colin Meurk and BDP, 2015

After the September 2010 Christchurch earthquake, a damaging but less destructive event than the 'quake of February 2011, the city council asked the public for ideas to inform the development of a central city recovery plan. More than 100,000 suggestions were submitted, and the strong desire for a 'greener', more accessible and more engaging city found expression in the plan. A few months later, the plan was redundant and the consultative process that shaped it was replaced by a top-down planning regime imposed by central government via the Canterbury Earthquake Recovery Authority (CERA). The new direction for Christchurch redevelopment was set out in a 'blueprint', produced to meet a 100-day CERA deadline, that compressed the size of the CBD, thereby protecting property values — post-earthquake demolition was leaving a lot of empty lots — and divided the city into precincts centred on 'anchor' projects. One development sector is the 'East Frame'; to it was assigned the function 'play', and its anchor project is the 1.6-hectare playground sited between Armagh Street and a stretch of the Avon River. 'Deliberate but managed risk' was the concept for the 'all ages, all abilities' Margaret Mahy Family Playground, which was designed by Opus International Consultants (et al.) and named for the noted New Zealand author of children's books. The facility is popular, and it also did its bit for the property sector: the playground cost $3 million; the land it occupies, $20 million.

New Regent Street

Henry Francis Willis, 1932
Historic Place Category 1

In an architecturally serious city in which the bar was set early, and high, by Benjamin Mountfort's High Victorian Gothic Revivalism, New Regent Street is a surprising incidence of design levity. Along its 100-metre length the street is lined with two-storeyed, pastel-coloured terraced shops, alternately topped by a curly gable or a straight-edged canopy. It looks make-believe — a film set, perhaps, or a piece of townscape conceived by Disney imagineers. This fantastical quality is not accidental. The designer of New Regent Street was Henry Francis Willis (1892/93–1972), a Christchurch architect who specialised in cinemas. Willis brought his theatrical sensibility to the design of New Regent Street, and also a determination to give the project, which was developed as a kind of outdoor mall with 40 shops, a unifying coherence. These impulses combined in Willis's stylistic treatment of New Regent Street. He opted for Spanish Mission, which, after having been deployed sparingly for 20 years in New Zealand, enjoyed a sudden vogue, especially in Napier and Hasting as those cities were rebuilt after the 1931 earthquake. There's something sunny about the Spanish Mission style (it came from California, after all); in the midst of the Depression, it promised the welcome escapism of a movie from the Hollywood dream factory. After the 2011 earthquake, Fulton Ross Team Architects directed the street's restoration (2013).

Isaac Theatre Royal

145 Gloucester Street

Alfred and Sidney Luttrell, 1908
Historic Place Category 1

The Theatre Royal is the third incarnation of a theatre of this name on Gloucester Street and the second on this site. It was commissioned from the Australian-born and -trained Luttrell brothers, Alfred (1865–1924), who was the designer in the family, and Sidney (1872–1932), who supervised construction and dealt with clients. In this case, the client was a syndicate, headed by American actor and impresario James Cassius Williamson (1845–1913), that owned a chain of theatres in Australia and New Zealand. The Theatre Royal was retro, even in 1908: the Luttrell brothers took a form-advertises-function approach and styled the building in a theatrical Victorian manner. In the late 1920s the building was turned into a cinema, but in the 1950s it once more became a performance venue, serving up, for several decades, a democratic bill of fare — operas, ballets, concerts, wrestling matches, magic shows. A public campaign saved the building from demolition in the late 1970s and it was restored as a working theatre in 2004–2005 and again, far more substantially, after the 2010 and 2011 earthquakes (Warren and Mahoney Architects, lead architect Richard McGowan, 2014). A feature of the Rococo interior of the theatre, which now bears the name of civic benefactor Diana Isaac (1921–2012), is the dome with its original decoration — scenes from *A Midsummer Night's Dream*, painted by G. C. Post of Wellington's Carrara Ceiling Company, channelling his inner Tiepolo.

Tūranga

60 Cathedral Square

Architectus, Schmidt Hammer Lassen Architects and Matapopore Trust, 2018

In the first years of post-earthquake reconstruction there was considerable global interest in the questions of what form the new Christchurch central city might take and what sort of architecture might emerge on the *tabula rasa* of bulldozed city blocks. It seemed that this interest, and a steady parade of overseas experts, would yield a crop of buildings designed by international practices, and that a relatively parochial city could take on, for better or worse, a cosmopolitan architectural character. But this did not happen; apart from Shigeru Ban, whose presence was the result of peculiar circumstances (see pages 108–09), the only exotic architectural practice to have been involved in a major Christchurch recovery project is Schmidt Hammer Lassen Architects. The Danish firm is a world-leader in library architecture and, in partnership with Architectus and the Matapopore Trust, which represents local iwi Ngāi Tahu and hapū Ngāi Tūāhuriri, it designed Tūranga, the central Christchurch library. The anchor building is a five-storey civic marker on an important site that, pre-earthquake, was shared, in desultory fashion, by God (via ChristChurch Cathedral) and Mammon (in the guise of various tourist traps). Tūranga is a milestone in the evolution of bi-culturalism in a city in which Anglocentrism has at times blurred into racial chauvinism. The library acknowledges local iwi not only in its title — Tūranga is the name of a Ngāi Tahu ancestral settlement — but also through the realisation, most obvious in the library's dramatic and generous central stairway, of the concept of whakamanuhiri, the welcoming or 'bringing-in' of visitors.

ROUTE 5: NORTH SIDE

Two of the most significant buildings in Christchurch were designed, at a 100-year interval, by the city's most prominent architects: the Provincial Government Buildings (Benjamin Mountfort) and the Town Hall (Miles Warren). Both were badly damaged in the 2010–2011 earthquakes, and while the Provincial Buildings will not be restored for years, Christchurch Town Hall is now, after a profound reconstruction, as good as new. This route also includes a couple of religious buildings indicating that Anglicanism wasn't the only confessional game in an Anglophile town, and apartments by Peter Beaven that remind us that Miles Warren wasn't the only Christ's College old boy with a way with concrete blocks.

Knox Church

Corner 28 Bealey Avenue and Victoria Street

Robert William England, 1902;
Wilkie + Bruce Architects, 2014
Historic Place Category 2

Following the earthquakes of 2010 and 2011, scores of damaged historic buildings in Christchurch were demolished with an alacrity that heritage advocates condemned as opportunism. However, not all owners of distressed old buildings reached for the wrecker's ball; many committed to salvage solutions that ranged from partial restoration to total reconstruction. Knox Church as it now exists is near the latter end of this conservation spectrum. The Presbyterian church, which opened in 1902, was a brick and stone building designed in the Gothic Revival style by Robert William England (1863–1908), a talented architectural all-rounder who designed commercial buildings, Protestant churches and significant private houses, such as McLean's Mansion (see pages 136–37). The exterior of Knox Church was badly damaged in the 2011 earthquake and subsequently deconstructed. With its outside gone, the building's surviving interior woodwork — dark and rich — was revealed for all to see, and for several years the rimu roof trusses, beams and columns supporting the church's many gables made for a spectacular revelation of Gothicness. In this condition, the building made an evocative ruin, but of course the Presbyterians wanted to return their flagship church to its function. Wilkie + Bruce Architects (design architect Alun Wilkie, 1949–2017) retained the wonderful interior, wrapping it in a pointy-gabled copper and glass shell, supported by concrete buttresses and topped with a corrugated steel roof.

Victoria Clock Tower

Victoria and Montreal Streets

Benjamin Mountfort, 1860 (addition of base 1897; relocated 1930)
Historic Place Category 1

In the late 1850s, Christchurch's great Gothic Revival architect Benjamin Mountfort (1825–1898) designed a clock tower to sit on top of the first section of his Canterbury Provincial Government Buildings (see pages 130–31) on Durham Street. The problem was that the tower was made of iron and the building was made of wood. When the clock tower, packed into 147 boxes, arrived in New Zealand in 1860 from the Coventry foundry of Francis Skidmore (1817–1896) — an accomplished Gothic Revival metalworker — it was obviously too heavy to take its appointed place. The tower, without its clock, spent decades in a council storage yard until the city's leaders, in a typical colonial marriage of patriotism and pragmatism, re-purposed it as a monument marking the 1897 Diamond Jubilee of Queen Victoria. Local architecture practice Strouts and Ballantyne designed a stone base for the tower which, finally reunited with its clock, was erected on the corner of Manchester, High and Lichfield Streets. On this site the tower later became a traffic hazard, and after rejecting an offer from Hamilton City Council to buy it, in 1930 Christchurch City Council moved it to its present location where it was restored after the 2011 earthquake. Unfortunately, at some time in its history the tower lost the gold leaf that originally covered its wrought iron railings.

Christchurch Law Courts

Durham Street North and Armagh Street

Government Architect's Office, MoW, 1978–1989

The Christchurch Law Courts is a project that went on
for so long its progress seems explicable only in terms of
Newtonian physics, specifically the law defining the inertia
of objects once set in motion. Which is another way of saying
the building was a job of the New Zealand Ministry of Works
(MoW). The MoW did a huge amount of work last century
but, partly because its schedule was subject to political
whim, it took its time in doing so. When the Christchurch
Law Courts was finally completed in 1989 (with a single
tower, not the planned two), one of its architects, Gordon
Cullinan, reportedly said he had been working on the
building for 21 years. What this meant is that when it was
finished it already seemed anachronistic. If it had been built
when it was designed, the Brutalist building would have been
part of the Christchurch Modernist architectural family, a
sibling to buildings at Canterbury University's Ilam campus
(see pages 144–59). The design intentions were admirable.
MoW architects made respectful reference to the adjacent
Christchurch Town Hall (see pages 132–35), formally, in the
cantilever of the low-rise administration block (1978), and
materially in the concrete aggregate which both projects
sourced from the same quarry. The Christchurch Law Courts
has a great riverside site; the building wasn't cheap — quality
concrete, copper roofs — and it's very strong. But it is empty
now, and unloved, and no one seems to know quite what to
do with it.

Canterbury Provincial Government Buildings

280 Durham Street North, Armagh Street and Gloucester Street

Benjamin Mountfort, 1858–1865
Historic Place Category 1

In architecture, as in everything else, achievement depends on both talent and timing. In colonial Christchurch, Benjamin Mountfort (1825–1898) had the opportunity to make the most of his ability, and he took it, designing numerous significant buildings in the course of a long career that established his reputation as the city's architectural founding father. Mountfort arrived in Christchurch from England in 1850 as a young Gothic Revival architect, and his great good fortune was that the style in which he was so proficient endured locally until his death. In the late 1850s, Mountfort and his brother-in-law Isaac Luck (1817–1881) were the official architects for the Canterbury settlement when they received the plum commission to design a building to house the Provincial Council. The job turned into a three-stage project, expanding with Canterbury's increasing wealth. The initial timber building, centred on a council chamber modelled on late medieval English manorial halls, soon received an extension featuring a stone tower, and in 1865 — by which time Mountfort was briefly in partnership with Maxwell Bury (1825–1912) — a stone council chamber was added. This dramatic chamber, with its encaustic tiles, sandstone walls and stained glass windows from the London firm of Lavers & Barraud, was to become Mountfort's most acclaimed work. Along with the central stone tower, it was destroyed in the 2011 earthquake; much of the timber structure survives.

Christchurch Town Hall

86 Kilmore Street

Warren and Mahoney, 1972; restored 2019
Historic Place Category 1

Christchurch Town Hall is so synonymous with Miles Warren
you'd think he was destined to design it. Not quite, however:
the commission for the design of what was only the second
post-Second World War town hall in New Zealand was the
result of a competition, a 58-entry contest that legend
has conflated into a showdown between the two largest
personalities in Christchurch post-war architecture, Warren
and Peter Beaven. (In fact, Beaven's submission did not even
make it onto the shortlist of five finalists.) But Warren really
wanted the job, and why not? To design the most important
civic building in your own city is an architect's dream, and
Warren knew what the Christchurch Town Hall could mean
for his firm, his career and his reputation. The phone call
in June 1966, informing him of his competition win, was
time-stopping. 'Taking that call,' Warren wrote, 40 years
later, 'remains the most exciting moment of my life.' Now
we can see that Christchurch Town Hall was the apogee of
Warren's career. The Town Hall is not a singular building, but
rather a composition of structures — the wonderful main
auditorium (one of the best rooms in New Zealand); smaller
concert chamber; banquet hall; restaurant; and meeting
rooms — in a disciplined Modernist palette of concrete,
timber and plate glass, with brass fittings, a copper roof and
Carrara marble, sparingly used. Warren's design skills were
complemented by Maurice Mahoney's talent for detailing
and documentation, builder Chas Luney's experience
of construction in Christchurch, and Harold Marshall's
mastery of acoustics. Christchurch Town Hall was the career
springboard for Marshall (b. 1931), who went on to build an
international reputation as an acoustic architect; in his late
career, he worked with the Pritzker Prize–winning architect

Jean Nouvel on the Paris Philharmonie (2015). Christchurch Town Hall was severely damaged in the 2010–2011 earthquakes but, thanks to a victory of local democracy over central government preference, was — expensively — restored by Warren and Mahoney Architects instead of being, even more expensively, replaced. The building now sits on an 850-millimetre concrete raft slab, which is itself supported by more than a thousand concrete piles injected or 'jet grouted' eight metres into the ground.

Christchurch Town Hall, Kilmore Street.

McLean's Mansion

387 Manchester Street

Robert and William England, 1902
Historic Place Category 1

Small farmers were a core constituency of the Liberal Party which governed New Zealand from 1891 to 1912, and the break-up of large landholdings was one of the party's principal policies. Through a variety of measures, more carrot than stick, the proprietors of 'big estates' were encouraged to relinquish much of their extensive acreage. One landowner persuaded to take a government cash offer was Allan McLean (1822–1907), a self-made Scot who had accumulated capital on the Victorian goldfields before settling in Canterbury and investing in land. With the proceeds of the sale of his Waikakahi station — around $60 million in today's money — McLean commissioned a city house, Holly Lea (now McLean's Mansion), from the practice of the England brothers, Robert William (1863–1908) and Edward Herbert (1875–1949). Robert England, who seems to have been the firm's design director, was stylistically agnostic (see Knox Church, pages 124–25). If the 53-roomed, twin-towered McLean's Mansion, one of New Zealand's largest timber houses, belongs to a tradition, it's nineteenth-century English 'Jacobethan'. Historian Melanie Lovell-Smith says the design references the Rothschild's country house Mentmore Towers (Joseph Paxton, 1854); Harlaxton Manor (Anthony Salvin, 1837) could be another antecedent. McLean was old when his house was built; he bequeathed it as a home 'for women of education and refinement in reduced or straightened circumstances' and so it functioned for half a century. The house is currently under repair.

St Mary's Apartments

868 Colombo Street

Peter Beaven, 1997

Memorable architectural encounters do not have to involve buildings. For years, one of the best experiences in New Zealand architecture was a conversation with Peter Beaven (1925–2012). Beaven was eloquent and opinionated but sufficiently reasonable — when not on a public stage — to inoculate his pronouncements with a nuanced subtext. He didn't like Modernism, but distinguished between doctrinaire Corbusier and humanist Aalto; he often opposed schemes championed by his Christchurch contemporary Miles Warren, but always acknowledged Warren's design talent; he disdained privilege, but recognised its advantages — his time at Christ's College taught him, he said, that 'you could do what you liked as long as you did it with panache'. What Beaven really liked, and advocated for, was the architectural tradition of Christchurch, and in particular the work of Benjamin Mountfort. 'Without him I wouldn't live in Christchurch,' he said, and he meant it. Beaven's office was in Mountfort's Provincial Government Buildings (see pages 130–31); after the building collapsed in the 2011 earthquake, Beaven left the city. Thankfully, his St Mary's Apartments, named for the convent that formerly occupied the site, survived the quake. In its design, the 72-unit complex alludes to the courtyards and steep roofs of The Arts Centre and Christ's College; in its structure, it refers to the concrete blockwork popularised in Warren's early architecture; in its layout, it demonstrates Beaven's command of multi-unit planning.

St Mary's Convent (Rose) Chapel

866 Colombo Street

S & A Luttrell, 1910
Historic Place Category 2

St Mary's Convent Chapel is the surviving building of a Catholic enclave established in Anglican Christchurch in the late nineteenth century. The chapel, now deconsecrated and operated as a venue for hire, is testament to the drive and determination of Irish nun Margaret Boland — or Mother Mary Mechtildes, to use her Sisters of Mercy religious title — who bought land on Colombo Street and built a convent and school. When it came time to add a chapel, Mother Mary Mechtildes, it seems, knew what she wanted: something like the chapel at her order's convent in Handsworth, Birmingham, designed by the Gothic Revival architect Augustus Pugin (1812–1852), and featuring windows made by Birmingham's Hardman & Co stained glass works. The practice of Australian-born brothers Sidney (1872–1932) and Alfred Luttrell (1865–1924), which became a preferred supplier to the Christchurch Catholic Diocese and, quite compatibly, the horse-racing industry, designed the chapel, specifying Ōamaru stone and Hoon Hay basalt, and Hardman stained glass windows. The chapel narrowly escaped demolition after the Sisters of Mercy quit the site in 1993, and was badly damaged in the 2011 earthquake. Dave Pearson Architects put the building back together again, sensitively restoring its elements, including the rose window from which the chapel takes its current name.

ROUTE 6: ILAM CAMPUS

The Ilam campus of the University of Canterbury is a bit out of the way — although just 15 minutes from the city centre by bus — but is well worth a visit for its extant collection of Modernist buildings. The university moved from the city to its suburban site 60 years ago, at a time when Modernist planning and Brutalist architecture promised to be the means to realise a brave new world. Miles Warren's College House is a masterpiece of New Zealand Modernism, and the campus also features strong work by other mid-century Christchurch architects, and more recent work in a contemporary vein.

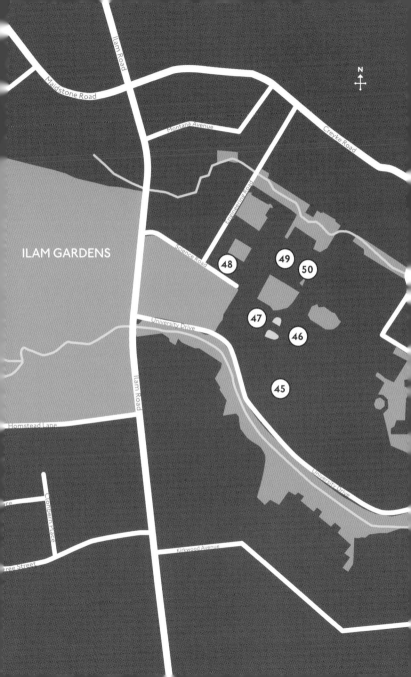

Ilam Campus,
University of Canterbury

The Ilam campus of the University of Canterbury represents one of the most pronounced shifts in New Zealand architectural history: a pivot from Mountfortian Gothic Revivalism to Corbusian Modernism. In 1949, after several years of rapid roll growth, Canterbury College, as the public university was then known, decided to move from the inner city to the western fringe of suburbia. Since the late nineteenth century, the College had been housed in the cluster of Gothic Revival buildings that now constitute the Christchurch Arts Centre. The new location was a 76-hectare site 5 kilometres away. Architectural responsibility for the redevelopment was assumed by the office of the Government Architect, which for most of the 1950s was led by Gordon Wilson (1900–1959), a key figure in New Zealand Modernist architecture. The migration to Ilam, broadly understood, was from an Oxbridge collegiate arrangement of buildings, more a result of sympathetic accretion than master-planning zeal, to a campus layout guided by Modernist zoning principles that grouped buildings by function: teaching, dwelling, social life. The result, from the early 1960s to the mid-1970s, under the leadership of Assistant Government Architect John Blake-Kelly (1913–1988), was a flourishing of concrete Brutalism on the flat, green fields of Canterbury, very similar to the development model pursued by the new provincial universities of post-war Britain. Brutalism is history now, but Ilam's Modernist buildings still make strong statements and a challenge for contemporary architects in how to respond to them.

College House

Warren and Mahoney, 1965–1970
Historic Place Category 1

In 1964 Miles Warren received a brief for a new project: 'a college for 120 men'. It wasn't a lot to go on, but from it came one of the outstanding works in New Zealand architecture. As Warren later wrote, the key word in the economical instruction was 'college'. The Anglican student hall of residence was not to be a mere dormitory, but a complete community, with bedrooms, common rooms and dining hall, and later a chapel and library. So, no march of rooms along either side of a corridor, with toilets at the end. Instead: eight three-storey 'sets' with five bedrooms on each floor, all grouped around a staircase. These sets flank two sides — five on one side, three on the other — of an Oxbridge-style quadrangle closed at opposite ends by the dining hall and library; the chapel pushes into the quad on its three-set side. College House is a product of what Warren called modern architecture's 'constructivist' phase, a term that evokes the spectre of Bolshevik machine-age art and architecture. This was perhaps not quite what Christ's College old boy Warren had in mind, but you can see what he was getting at. With its programmatic clarity and disciplined and frugal deployment of straightforward materials and fittings — load-bearing concrete blocks; fair-face concrete; timber beams; plywood; Rietveld-like furniture — College House combines the key Modernist precept, form follows function, with Warren's particular brand of explicatory Brutalism. Constructionalism, you could call it, with a side-order of homage in the Gothic allusion of the pointy M-shaped copper roofs of the chapel and library, and the references in the trusses and beams of the chapel to Cecil Wood's Memorial Dining Room at Christ's College (see pages 56–57).

College House, University of Canterbury, Ilam campus.

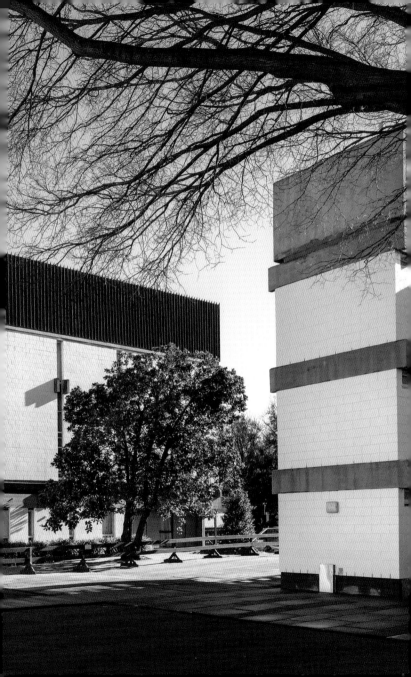

Angus Tait Building

Hall and Mackenzie, 1966

The Computer Centre, now re-named for electronics pioneer Angus Tait (1919–2017), was designed to house a telephone exchange and a computer (just the one, sixties big and slow). In comparison with its Brutalist campus siblings it is a modest and graceful building — you could even say it was better than it needed to be (a sure test for good architecture). The building is real Modernists' Modernism: propped up on piers, with a cantilever, a butterfly roof and sun-shading concrete fins on the long elevations. On its greenfield site, the Computer Centre looked fresh and very contemporary when completed, and it retains much of its distinction in what has become a less sympathetic context. The building was designed by the practice of Humphrey Hall (1912–1988) and Keith Hamilton Mackenzie (1920–1987). The prominence of Warren and Mahoney has overshadowed other Christchurch Modern-era practices; the firm of Hall and Mackenzie doesn't deserve obscurity. Unlike Christchurch architects of an earlier generation, and some of their peers, who were stylistically heterodox, Hall and Mackenzie seem to have spent their careers as faithful Modernists. Hall designed for himself, when still in his twenties, one of the first truly Modernist houses in New Zealand, the Corbusian Humphrey Hall House (1938) in Timaru. After the war, several years of which he spent in a German prisoner-of-war camp, Hall was in practice for a decade with Paul Pascoe, and then with Keith Mackenzie, who had spent his early twenties commanding a naval patrol boat in the Pacific theatre of war.

Puaka–James Hight Building

Government Architect's Office, MoW, 1974

The 11-storey Brutalist behemoth that is the Puaka–James Hight Building is, at 53 metres high, the tallest building on the Ilam campus, and one of the heftiest extant examples of the mid-century concrete Modernism of the Ministry of Works (MoW). It was designed as the University of Canterbury's main library and it continues to serve that function, although it has always housed other university departments and services as well. The building, initially named for humanities professor and university administrator James Hight (1870–1958) and latterly given the Māori name for Rigel, the brightest star in the Orion constellation, was commissioned from the MoW in 1963. Typically, construction was delayed as the government reshuffled its spending priorities. Local builder Charles Luney (1905–2006) — Modernism's maker in Christchurch — got started in 1969, and the building finally opened in 1974. John Blake-Kelly had responsibility in the Government Architect's Office for Ilam campus through the 1960s, but Roger Warr (1931–2011) seems to have led the James Hight project. Like any sizeable Brutalist building, Puaka–James Hight is confronting, and there have been attempts to use planting to soften its appearance. In the 1980s, ivy was grown on Ilam's Brutalist façades, against the inclinations of the grounds superintendent who noted that the whole point of Brutalism was to see the concrete. At Puaka–James Hight, the cover-up was discontinued when ivy grew into the heating ducts. The post-earthquake rehabilitation of the Puaka–James Hight Building included an extensive re-working of the undercroft by Warren and Mahoney Architects (2013).

Matariki (Registry Building)

Hall and Mackenzie, 1974

Aside from College House, the Registry Building — now called Matariki, the Māori name for the Pleiades star cluster and also for the New Year — might be the outstanding work of Modernist architecture on the Ilam campus. The west face of the building is especially compelling. Thin pillars of concrete, more fins than columns, exaggerate the height of the building beyond its six storeys, and are complemented by tall trees rising from the lawn. The composition shows how good Brutalist buildings can look in a park setting. Sections of the top floor, which houses the offices of university administrators, project from the building like bartizan turrets on medieval castles. These features, and the general staunchness of the Registry Building, have encouraged conjecture that the building was designed as a fortress to repel student invaders. This seems improbable — the University of Canterbury campus in the early 1970s was hardly the Sorbonne in May '68 — although students have staged the occasional occupation over the years. The Registry Building demonstrates Hall and Mackenzie's mastery of concrete design, the signature characteristic of the so-called Christchurch School over the two decades from the late 1950s. Like other Brutalist work on the Ilam campus, the building could be viewed as an in-your-face proclamation of local architectural ability directed at a university that never established a School of Architecture. The Registry Building was badly damaged in the 2011 earthquake; structural remediation and internal 'modernisation' was supervised by Warren and Mahoney Architects (2014).

ROUTE 6–47

Jack Erskine Building

Architectus, with Cook, Sargisson Hitchcock and Royal Associates, 1998

When it opened in 1998, the Mathematics, Statistics and Computer Sciences Building, now named for scientist and engineer Jack Erskine (1872–1960), was the best work of architecture at Ilam since College House. It probably still is. In its materials and their monumental deployment, it relates to the Modernist buildings constructed in the first 20 years of the campus's development, but if architecture is a dialogue, you could say the Maths, Stats and Computer Sciences Building significantly advanced the conversation. The building was designed by a team led by Architectus, a practice established in Auckland in the late 1980s by Patrick Clifford, Malcolm Bowes and Michael Thomson. It is tempting to see in the building a fusion of two architectural traditions: the post-war, temperate-climate architecture of Auckland, thinner skinned and more open to the natural environment; and the heavier architecture of Christchurch, thick-walled and more closed against a less amenable climate. In its legible distinction between three north-facing, seven-storey towers housing staff offices, a four-storey teaching wing to the south, and the circulation areas connecting them, the building is a model of clarity; its refinement stands out against its Brutalist forebears like pin-stripes among rugby-jersey hoops. Architectural spectators of the building will appreciate a separation of 'served' and 'servant' spaces typical of the work of the great American architect Louis Kahn (1901–1974). For their part, inhabitants of the building have had reason to be grateful for its efficient environmental performance.

Ernest Rutherford Building

Jasmax, 2018

What do buildings say about the practices that designed
them? Over the past 20 years, Jasmax and Warren and
Mahoney Architects have emerged as New Zealand's two
largest architectural firms, with offices in several cities
around the country, and in Warren and Mahoney's case, also
in Australia. Jasmax originated and is still based in Auckland;
Warren and Mahoney expanded from its Christchurch office.
Without engaging in geographical determinism, it is possible
to discern in the practices' architecture traits associated
with their places of origin. While Jasmax is increasingly
corporate, the firm's architecture traditionally has been more
relaxed than that of Warren and Mahoney, which is given to
producing assertive and even dominating buildings. Jasmax
hasn't had a house style, but in the four decades following its
foundation in 1963 its work has been characterised by a kind
of humanism that has softened the hard edges of modern
architecture. Conveniently, the firms' cultural differences are
illustrated by adjacent terminals at Christchurch Airport: one
hard and bright, by Warren and Mahoney (with Australian firm
Hassell); the other more layered and subdued, by Jasmax
(with Australian firm BVN). Jasmax's approach suits the recent
vogue for flexible commercial and education spaces and is
represented on the Ilam campus by the sciences building
named for Canterbury University's most famous alumnus,
nuclear physicist Ernest Rutherford (1871–1937). The key to
the building's planning is the grand atrium, which is all about
ascent, literally and metaphorically — the design is intended
to evoke Tāwhaki's journey into the heavens.

Beatrice Tinsley Building

Jasmax, DJRD Architects
and Royal Associates Architects, 2019

After the Christchurch earthquakes, it seemed popular sentiment for change would find profound structural expression, both at the scale of individual buildings and of the city. It hasn't really worked out that way. New buildings are far more resilient than their pre-quake predecessors, and there is little appetite for high-rise habitation in what was anyway a comparatively low-rise city. But most new buildings in Christchurch don't look much different from new buildings in other places, or from each other, and the procrustean planning regime — Modernism redux, with zones recast as 'precincts' — imposed by the recovery authority foreclosed the possibilities of new paradigms of urban development. The story of post-quake, non-residential timber construction in Christchurch shows how hard it can be to give architectural realisation to ideas whose time would seem to have come. You would think timber might indeed be the natural choice for the rebuilding of a New Zealand city: intuitively, it seems 'safe'; it is a plentiful and sustainable material; and we're used to working with it. Also, in Christchurch, the University of Canterbury carries out world-leading research in timber engineering. But the gap between technological understanding, on the one hand, and manufacturing and building capability and political commitment, on the other, means large-scale timber structures are rather like demonstration models. One such exemplar is the Ilam building named for acclaimed astronomer and cosmologist Beatrice Tinsley (1941–1981). The four-storey building uses laminated veneer lumber (LVL) beams, 'moment-framed' and cross-braced, to provide flexible resistance to severe seismic movement.

A NOTE ABOUT ARCHITECTURAL STYLES

Art Deco: Architectural and design style popular in the 1920s and 1930s that took its name from the 1925 Exposition Internationale des Arts Décoratifs et Industriels Modernes in Paris. In architecture, Art Deco was a highly stylised version of Modernism that blended sleek forms, contemporary materials and bold colours to self-consciously glamorous effect.

Arts and Crafts: Design philosophy and practice that emerged in Britain in the mid-nineteenth century and was influential in the decades prior to the First World War. Arts and Crafts architecture evoked the organic nature and functional simplicity of pre-Industrial Age architecture and, as its name suggests, promoted handcrafted construction and the 'honest' use of natural materials.

Beaux-Arts: The rich Classically-influenced architecture style promulgated by the École des Beaux-Arts in Paris from the mid-nineteenth century through the first few decades of the twentieth century.

Brutalism: Term coined in Britain in the early 1950s — derived from 'béton brut' (raw concrete) — to characterise the Modernist architecture of Le Corbusier and applied to monolithic poured-concrete buildings with clearly expressed or emphasised structural elements. The style, also known as 'New Brutalism', endured in New Zealand until the end of the 1970s.

Classical architecture or Classicism: The revival of, or reference to, Greek or Roman architecture of classical antiquity. A serious architecture of pedestals, columns and pediments, and decorative restraint.

Collegiate Gothic: Sub-genre of Gothic Revival architecture popular in the late nineteenth and early twentieth centuries on school and university campuses. The historicist style blended Gothic and Tudor elements and often favoured a more horizontal expression of Gothic Revival's vertical or 'pointy' forms.

Gothic Revival: The nineteenth-century revival, associated in Britain with High Church Anglicanism and Roman Catholicism, of the Gothic architectural style dominant in much of late medieval Europe. The Gothic style was an architecture of pointy bits — spires, flying buttresses, steep gables, rib vaults and lancet windows. Gothic Revivalism came to Christchurch with the Anglican settlers of the Canterbury Association, and held sway for the first 50 years of the city's history.

Italianate, Italian Renaissance, Italian Villa: Synonymous terms for the picturesque adaptation of the Italian Renaissance Villa type popular in nineteenth-century Britain, especially among nouveau riche bourgeois clients; the style spread to the British Empire and North America, where it lingered until the end of the century.

Jacobethan or Jacobethan Revival: Term originated in the 1930s by English poet John Betjeman to describe a nineteenth-century revival style that combined elements of Elizabethan and Jacobean architecture. Features included wide 'Tudor' arches, steep gables, porches, parapets and chimneys, and lighter stone surrounds for doors and windows.

Moderne: Also called Streamline Moderne, a toned-down iteration of Art Deco that emerged in the 1930s and was characterised by curved forms and horizontal lines, and often by ship-like styling and nautical elements.

Modernism: The most important architectural style or movement of the twentieth century. Modernism was characterised by a rejection of ornamentation, the belief that a building's form should follow from an analysis of its function, and a commitment to the rational use of contemporary industrial materials and building technologies. In New Zealand, after a slow start, Modernism was the architectural orthodoxy from the Second World War to the end of the 1970s.

Neo-Georgian: Revival in early twentieth-century Britain, and therefore in New Zealand, of the architectural style in vogue under the Hanoverian monarchs, Georges I to IV (spanning 1714–1830). A restrained style, both in its original as well as its revived iterations, characterised by symmetry, balance and proportion. Brick and stone were materials typical of the style.

Palazzo: A style of late nineteenth- and early twentieth-century building based on the town houses (palazzi) of Italian Renaissance patrician families. The building type — solid and symmetrical, and more austere than buildings in 'Italian Villa' mode — was particularly popular with late-Victorian London gentlemen's clubs.

Queen Anne Revival: A late nineteenth- and early twentieth-century historicist architectural style that referred very loosely to the English Baroque style popular in the reign of Queen Anne (1702–1714). Features could include gables, turrets and fine brickwork with bands of masonry detailing.

Romanesque: Pre-Gothic style of medieval architecture featuring semi-circular arches for windows and doors, vaults to support the roof, and massive piers and walls.

Spanish Mission: An early twentieth-century architectural style derived from late eighteenth- and early nineteenth-century Spanish colonial buildings in California. The style, characterised by stucco walls with a curvilinear gable shape or low parapets at the roof line, enjoyed some popularity in New Zealand in the inter-war period.

Tudor Revival: An early twentieth-century revival of the late-Gothic architectural style of Tudor England incorporating towers, mock battlements and crenellations, oriel windows, and low 'Tudor' arches that had some popularity as a New World collegiate architectural style. Its suburban domestic variant communicated antique rusticity through the use of half-timber work and gabled roofs.

GLOSSARY OF ARCHITECTURAL TERMS

Bartizan: An overhanging, wall-mounted turret projecting from the walls of medieval and early modern fortifications and used for surveillance and defensive purposes.

Buttress: Masonry mass projecting from or built against a wall to provide support; a flying buttress is an arch or half-arch that extends from the upper part of a wall to a pier, again to counter a building's lateral thrust.

Chancel: The space around the altar at the east end of a church, traditionally reserved for the clergy and choir.

Encaustic (tiles): Tiles into which colours have been set in a heating process.

Entabulature: Upper part of a Classical building, supported by columns, and comprising the architrave (the lintel above the columns), frieze (the decorative band above the architrave), and cornice (the horizontal moulding at the top of a building).

Festoon: Carved building-façade ornament in the form of a ribboned garland of fruit and flowers.

Fenestration: The arrangement of windows in a building.

Finial: An ornament, commonly foliated, on the top of a building.

Fritted glass: Glass printed with a ceramic composite that has been fired into an opaque coating.

Hipped roof: A roof which slopes downwards on all four sides towards a building's walls.

Ionic column: One of the three column styles of Greek Classical architecture, more slender than the Doric and less ornate than the Corinthian column.

Moment framing: Structural technique designed to allow a building to withstand seismic shocks. Rigid framing connections are used to lock together a flexible building frame resistant to lateral and overturning forces.

Mullioned: Windows divided by vertical bars or piers, usually of stone.

Oriel window: A type of bay window that protrudes from the main wall of a building, usually from an upper floor, and is supported by a corbel (a structural element, usually of stone) or bracket.

Parapet: An extension of a wall along the edge of the roof, originally designed for defensive purposes.

Pediment: Classically derived gable, usually triangular in shape, surmounting the entabulature of a building above the main entrance.

Pilaster: A protruding rectangular column or pier.

Portico: Covered building entrance, usually a roof supported by columns.

Quoin: A dressed stone at the corner of a building.

String course: A decorative horizontal band, usually of brick or stone, on a building façade.

Transepts: Transverse arms of a cross-shaped church; that is, the two areas that flank, on either side, the nave or main body of the building.

Undercroft: Traditionally, a cellar or storage room, often vaulted; in contemporary usage, a ground or street level area, open at the side but covered by the building above.

CONNECTIONS

Alvar Aalto (1898–1976): Influential Finnish architect and designer whose Modernist buildings exhibit humane qualities and were realised as 'total works of art'; that is, he and his first wife, Aino Aalto (1894–1949), would design not only a building but also its fittings and furniture.

Richard Cromwell Carpenter (1812–1855): English architect who was closely involved with the Gothic Revival and in particular its application to Anglican church buildings.

Le Corbusier, born Charles-Édouard Jeanneret (1887–1965): Swiss-born architect, planner and polemicist who was probably the most famous architect of the twentieth century; designer of such canonical Modernist works as the Villa Savoye near Paris, Notre-Dame du Haut chapel at Ronchamps and the city of Chandigarh in northern India.

Frank Gehry (1929–): Canadian-born American architect who is famous for such virtuoso designs as the Guggenheim Bilbao (1997), Walt Disney Concert Hall (Los Angeles, 2003) and his own post-modern house in Santa Monica (California, 1978). Now so famous he is a corporate brand.

Walter Gropius (1883–1969): German architect who was a founder of the short-lived but hugely influential Bauhaus design school and one of the key figures in the development of Modernist architecture. Practised and taught in the United States after he fled from Nazi Germany in the mid-1930s.

Toyo Ito (1941–): Leading Japanese architect celebrated for his innovative designs and conceptual approach to his practice; awarded international architecture's leading personal award, the Pritzker Prize, in 2013.

Louis Kahn (1901–1974): Eminent American architect celebrated for designing buildings of monumental presence and authority such as the Salk Institute (La Jolla, California, 1959), National Assembly Building of Bangladesh (Dhaka, 1962), Phillips Exeter Academy Library (Fxeter, New Hampshire, 1965) and Kimbell Art Museum (Fort Worth, Texas, 1966).

Maya Lin (1959–): American artist and designer who was 21 years old when she won the 1981 competition to design the Vietnam Veterans Memorial in Washington DC, a project that has had a huge influence on memorial design around the world.

Edwin Lutyens (1869–1944): Celebrated as the leading English architect of his time; a traditionalist who was adept at adapting to contemporary establishment taste, he won numerous commissions for country houses and war memorials, and played an important part in the design of New Delhi.

Augustus Pugin (1812–1852): English architect, designer and critic who was a pioneer of the Gothic Revival; Catholic convert who designed many churches, both Anglican and Catholic, as well as the interior of the Palace of Westminster in London.

Gerrit Rietveld (1888–1964): Dutch architect and furniture designer; in both fields he focused on inexpensive production methods, new materials, prefabrication and standardisation, and to this day architects are covetous of his chair designs, especially that icon of Modernist design, the Red and Blue Chair (1917).

George Gilbert Scott (1811–1878): Prolific and influential English Gothic Revival architect; churches and cathedrals — including ChristChurch Cathedral in New Zealand — were specialties, although he also designed workhouses, asylums and such prominent secular structures as the Midland Grand

Hotel at St Pancras Station (London, 1873) and the Albert Memorial (London, 1876). His two sons, George Gilbert Scott Jr (1839–1897) and John Oldrid Scott (1841–1913), were also architects, as was, more successfully, his grandson Sir Giles Gilbert Scott (1880–1960).

William Van Alen (1883–1954): American big-building Modernist architect best known for designing the Chrysler Building (New York, 1930); a dispute over his fee with his client, car-maker Walter Chrysler, together with the onset of the Depression, derailed his architectural career and he turned to teaching sculpture for a living.

Ludwig Mies van der Rohe (1886–1969): One of the outstanding twentieth-century architects. Born in Germany, he designed one of the great early Modernist buildings, the Barcelona Pavilion (1929), and taught at the Bauhaus before moving in the late 1930s to America, where he designed the equally acclaimed Farnsworth House (Plano, Illinois, 1951) and Seagram Building (New York, 1958).

Frank Lloyd Wright (1867–1959): The greatest American architect, some claim, of all time. In a 70-year career lived in the public gaze, Wright designed hundreds of buildings and championed his 'organic' brand of modern architecture. Fallingwater (Mill Run, Pennsylvania, 1937) is hailed as one of the best-ever works of American architecture, and other significant Wright buildings are the Robie Residence (Chicago, Illinois, 1909), Taliesin West (Scottsdale, Arizona, 1937) and the Solomon R. Guggenheim Museum (New York, 1959).

FURTHER READING

For an overview of New Zealand's architectural history, see Peter Shaw's *A History of New Zealand Architecture* (3rd edition, Hodder Moa Beckett, 2003) — still the standard work, and a good place to start. The story of Māori architecture is covered in far more detail by Deidre Brown in *Māori Architecture: From Fale to Wharenui and Beyond* (Penguin, 2009). For a survey of much of the country's twentieth-century architecture, see Julia Gatley (ed), *Long Live the Modern: New Zealand's Architecture, 1904–1984* (Auckland University Press, 2008).

There are several monographs about Christchurch architects and architecture. Architectural historian Ian Lochhead recorded the life and work of the city's seminal nineteenth-century architect in *A Dream of Spires: Benjamin Mountfort and the Gothic Revival* (Canterbury University Press, 1999). Lochhead also edited *Peter Beaven: Architect* (Peter Beaven Architecture, 2016), a memoir written by one of Christchurch's outstanding later-twentieth-century architects. Miles Warren wrote about his architectural career and significant buildings in *Miles Warren: An Autobiography* (Canterbury University Press, 2008). The work of Christchurch's largest architecture firm is also presented in *Warren & Mahoney Architects, 1958–1989* (Warren and Mahoney, 1989) and *New Territory: Warren and Mahoney: 50 Years of New Zealand Architecture* (Balasoglou Books, 2005).

There aren't many books on individual New Zealand buildings, but Christchurch's post-earthquake recovery has generated three. The extraordinary story of the Christchurch Transitional Cathedral is told in *Shigeru Ban: Cardboard Cathedral* (Auckland University Press, 2014), by Andrew Barrie, who designed two of the buildings in this guide. Essays in *The Christchurch Town Hall 1965–2019* (Canterbury University Press, 2019), edited by Ian Lochhead, describe the gestation and reconstruction of the city's most important civic building. *St Andrew's College Centennial Chapel*, edited by John Walsh (Architectus Bowes Clifford Thomson, 2018), marked the completion of a significant new Christchurch building. (The chapel is just outside the central city area covered in this guide, but is well worth a visit.)

A pair of University of Canterbury doctoral theses provide much detail about two of the architects featured in this guide. George Penlington is one of the Christchurch school architects who figures in Murray Noel Williams' 'Building Yesterday's Schools: An Analysis of Educational Architectural Design as Practised by the Building Department of the Canterbury Education Board from 1916–1989' (2014), and Ruth Mary Helms produced the more succinctly titled 'The Architecture of Cecil Wood' (1996). An affinity for stained glass has been a Christchurch architectural trait since the city's Gothic Revival days, and its local use is chronicled with as much devotion as you could wish for in Fiona Ciaran's 1992 University of Canterbury PhD thesis, 'Stained Glass in Canterbury, New Zealand, 1860 to 1988'. (University of Canterbury theses may be downloaded from the online UC Research Repository.)

The New Zealand Heritage List Rārangi Kōrero, maintained by the government agency Heritage New Zealand Pouhere Taonga, is an invaluable source of information about New Zealand's significant buildings, and was very helpful in the preparation of this guide. The entries for nineteenth- and early twentieth-century buildings, and their architects, are particularly useful. One reason why it is often difficult to find out about mid- to late-twentieth-century New Zealand architecture is that few post-Second World War buildings have been accorded heritage — or 'Historic Place' — status, and therefore lack reliable accounts of their provenance.

Information about many of the architects in this guide can be found in *The Dictionary of New Zealand Biography*, which is now integrated into the online publication

Te Ara: The Encyclopedia of New Zealand. The well-written profiles in the *Dictionary* include short biographies of William Armson, Benjamin Mountfort, James Edward FitzGerald, William Gummer, Alfred and Sidney Luttrell, John Clarkson Madison, J. T. Mair, Paul Pascoe, Samuel Hurst Seager, Frederick Strouts and Cecil Wood.

The architecture section of Christchurch Libraries' website is a good source of information about the city's architects and architecture, and the website of Te Kāhui Whaihanga New Zealand Institute of Architects has some material on recent award-winning Christchurch buildings.

Finally, this guide has a predecessor: *Selected Architecture Christchurch: A Guide*, by Gavin Willis (The Caxton Press, 2005). That little book is now a rather sobering read; many of the buildings featured in the publication, which focused mainly on modern-era architecture, were casualties of the 2010–2011 earthquakes.

ACKNOWLEDGEMENTS

The publication of this guide has been supported by the Warren Trust, which does so much to promote architectural education, and by Te Kāhui Whaihanga New Zealand Institute of Architects and its Canterbury branch.

Most of the buildings in this guide were photographed from the street (which is how they will be viewed by the guide's users), but some were captured closer up. For access to grounds and buildings the author and photographer thank The Arts Centre Te Matatiki Toi Ora; Cathedral Grammar Junior School; Christ's College; Christchurch Botanic Gardens Visitor Centre; Christchurch City Libraries; College House; Oxford Terrace Baptist Church; the University of Canterbury; and Vbase (operator of Christchurch Town Hall).

Thanks to Nicola Legat for her ongoing commitment to publishing New Zealand architecture, to Imogen Greenfield for her design flair and attention to detail, and to Anna Bowbyes for her exemplary editorial and project management skills. Thanks to Sarah Rowlands, for stepping in at short notice and taking the photograph of Worcester Chambers (page 100).

And special thanks to Catherine Hammond, for her invaluable research assistance, advice and tolerance, and to Xavier Walsh, for his inspirational insouciance.

INDEX

Architects

Armson, William Barnett (1832/33–1883) 24, 29, 34, 47, 89

Ban, Shigeru 109, 121

Barrie, Andrew 59, 113

Beaven, Peter (1925–2012) 6, 7, 21, 75, 122, 132, 139

Blake-Kelly, John (1913–1988) 144, 151

Bowes, Malcolm 155

Bury, Maxwell (1825–1912) 131

Clifford, Patrick 155

Collins, John James (1855–1933) 7, 24, 34, 40, 47

Crisp, William Fitzjohn (1846–1924) 81

Dines, John Rayner (1927–1993) 75

England, Edward Herbert (1875–1949) 137

England, Robert William (1863–1908) 125, 137

FitzGerald, James Edward (1818–1896) 51

Gummer, William Henry (1884–1966) 71, 99

Hall, Humphrey (1912–1988) 6, 53, 149

Henning-Hansen, Holger (1921–1996) 75

Harman, Richard Dacre (1859–1927) 24, 34, 35, 40, 47

Lawry, Wilfred Melville (1894–1980) 65

Luck, Isaac (1817–1881) 131

Luttrell, Alfred (1865–1924) 119, 141

Luttrell, Sidney (1872–1932) 119, 141

Madison, Joseph Clarkson (1850–1923) 107

Mackenzie, Keith Hamilton (1920–1987) 149

Mahoney, Maurice (1929–2018) 67, 97, 132

Mair, John Thomas (1876–1959) 87

McGowan, Richard 119

Marshall, Harold 132

Minson, Stewart William (1904–2006) 75

Mountfort, Benjamin (1825–1898) 6, 20, 24, 31, 33, 39, 53, 55, 75, 81, 99, 105, 111, 122, 127, 131, 139

Mountfort, Cyril (1852–1920) 47, 55, 105

Pascoe, Paul (1908–1976) 6, 40, 53, 75, 149

Penlington, George (1865–1932) 15

Petre, Francis William (1847–1918) 7

Sanders, E. J. 113

Scott, George Gilbert (1811–1878) 105

Seager, Samuel Hurst (1855–1933) 24, 39, 99

Speechly, Robert (1840–1884) 6, 20, 53, 105

Strouts, Frederick (1834–1919) 81

Tezuka, Takahura and Yui 59

Thomson, Michael 155

Vezjak, Grega 69

Warr, Roger (1931–2011) 151

Warren, Miles 6, 7, 21, 40, 51, 57, 60, 67, 75, 97, 99, 122, 132, 139, 145

Watt, Trevor 17

Wilkie, Alun (1949–2017) 125

Wilson, Gordon (1900–1959) 144

Wood, Cecil Walter (1878–1947) 7, 24, 34, 40, 45, 47, 49, 53, 57, 99, 101

Willis, Henry Francis (1892/93–1972) 117

Architecture and design practices

Andrew Barrie Lab 59, 113

Architectus 93, 121, 155

Armson, Collins and Harman 47

Athfield Architects 17, 21, 63

BDP 115

Boffa Miskell 115

The Buchan Group 77

Canterbury Education Board 15

Collins and Harman 34, 39, 47

Cook Sargisson Hitchcock 155

Cox Architecture 91

DJRD Architects 159

Fulton Ross Team Architects 117

Government Architect/Ministry of Works 63, 87, 129, 144, 151

Gummer and Prouse 71

Hall and Mackenzie 149, 153

Jasmax 73, 95, 157, 159

LandLAB 115

Matapopore Trust 121

Minson, Henning-Hansen and Dines 75

NH Architecture 95

Opus Architecture 91

Opus International Consultants 115

Patterson Associates 19

Dave Pearson Architects 141

Royal Associates 155, 159

Schmidt Hammer Lassen Architects 121

Sheppard & Rout Architects 89

Stephenson & Turner 83

Strouts and Ballantyne 127

Tezuka Architects 59

Warren and Mahoney (later Warren and Mahoney Architects) 35, 67, 91, 97, 109, 111, 119, 132, 133, 145, 149, 151, 153

Wilkie + Bruce Architects 55, 125

Wilson & Hill Architects 85

Builders, craftspeople and consultants

Dyer, Tina 115

Frampton, George (1860–1928, sculptor) 99

Gurnsey, Frederick George (1868–1953, carver) 45, 49, 57, 71

Hardman & Co, also known as John Hardman Trading Co. (English stained glass and metalwork manufacturer) 141

Lavers & Barraud, later Lavers, Barraud and Westlake (English stained glass manufacturer) 131

Luney, Chas (1905–2006, builder) 132, 151

Meurk, Colin 115

Post, G. C. (scenic artist) 119

Skidmore, Francis (1817–1896, English Gothic Revival metalworker) 127

Wright, Edward George (1831–1902, engineer) 71

Buildings

151 Cambridge Terrace 73

65 Cambridge Terrace 67

77 Hereford Street 97

Angus Tait Building (Ilam Campus, University of Canterbury) 149

Ao Tawhiti Building 83

The Arts Centre Te Matatiki Toi Ora 24

Beatrice Tinsley Building (Ilam Campus, University of Canterbury) 159

Big School (Christ's College) 51

Bridge of Remembrance 71

Canterbury College Library (The Arts Centre Te Matatiki Toi Ora) 39

Canterbury Museum 20

Canterbury Provincial Government Buildings 131

'Cardboard' Cathedral 109

Cathedral Grammar Junior School 59

Chapel (Christ's College) 53

Chemistry Laboratory (The Arts Centre Te Matatiki Toi Ora) 34

Christchurch Art Gallery Te Puna o Waiwhetū 77

Christchurch Botanic Gardens Visitor Centre 19

Christchurch Boys' High School (The Arts Centre Te Matatiki Toi Ora) 29

ChristChurch Cathedral 105

Christchurch Club 111

Christchurch Law Courts 129

Christchurch Town Hall 132

Christ's College 40

Church of St Michael and All Angels, and Belfry 81

Clock Tower Block (The Arts Centre Te Matatiki Toi Ora) 31

College House (Ilam Campus, University of Canterbury) 145

Environment Canterbury Building 85

Ernest Rutherford Building (Ilam Campus, University of Canterbury) 157

Great Hall (The Arts Centre Te Matatiki Toi Ora) 33

Hagley Community College Main Building 15

Hagley Oval Pavilion 17

Hare Memorial Library (Christ's College) 49

Harper and Julius Houses (Christ's College) 55

Hine–Pāka Christchurch Bus Interchange 93

Ilam Campus, University of Canterbury 144

Isaac Theatre Royal 119

Jack Erskine Building (Ilam Campus, University of Canterbury) 155

Jacobs House (Christ's College) 45

Knox Church 125

Matariki (Ilam Campus, University of Canterbury) 153

McLean's Mansion 137

Memorial Dining Room (Christ's College) 57

Municipal Chambers — Our City Ōtautahi 99

New Regent Street 117

Oi Manawa Canterbury Earthquake National Memorial 69

Old Government Building 107

Oxford Terrace Baptist Church 113

Post and Telegraph Office 87

Puaka-James Hight Building (Ilam Campus, University of Canterbury) 151

School House (Christ's College) 47

St Mary's Apartments 139

St Mary's Convent (Rose) Chapel 141

Stranges and Glendenning Hill Building 89

Tākaro ā Poi Margaret Mahy Family Playground 115

Te Hononga Christchurch Civic Building 63

Te Omeka Justice and Emergency Services Precinct 91

The Terrace 95

Toi Moroki Centre of Contemporary Art (CoCA) Gallery 75

Tūranga 121

Victoria Clock Tower 127

West Avon Flats 65

Worcester Chambers 101

**MASSEY
UNIVERSITY
PRESS**

First published in 2020 by Massey University Press
Private Bag 102904, North Shore Mail Centre
Auckland 0745, New Zealand
www.masseypress.ac.nz

In association with:

Te Kāhui
Whaihanga
**New Zealand
Institute of
Architects**

Text copyright © John Walsh, NZIA Director Communications, 2020
Images © Patrick Reynolds, 2020, except for page 100 © Sarah Rowlands
Design by Imogen Greenfield, NZIA Manager Design and Creative, 2020

A catalogue record for this book is available from the National Library
of New Zealand

Printed and bound in China by 1010 Printing Asia Ltd

ISBN: 978-0-9951230-1-4

With the support of The Warren Trust

THE WARREN TRUST